Judicial Review of Administrative Discretion

Lex et Res Publica
Polish Legal and Political Studies

Edited by Anna Jaroń

Volume 10

Zur Qualitätssicherung und Peer Review der vorliegenden Publikation

Die Qualität der in dieser Reihe erscheinenden Arbeiten wird vor der Publikation durch die Herausgeberin der Reihe geprüft.

Notes on the quality assurance and peer review of this publication

Prior to publication, the quality of the work published in this series is reviewed by the editor of the series.

Adam Szot

Judicial Review of Administrative Discretion

The Influence of Court Decisions on Administrative Actions

PETER LANG

Bibliographic Information published by the Deutsche Nationalbibliothek
The Deutsche Nationalbibliothek lists this publication
in the Deutsche Nationalbibliografie; detailed bibliographic
data is available online at http://dnb.d-nb.de.

Library of Congress Cataloging-in-Publication Data
A CIP catalog record for this book has been applied for
at the Library of Congress.

This publication is a result of the research project No. 2013/11/N/HS5/04212 entitled "The influence of judicial decisions on the discretionary power of public administration in the law application processes" funded by the National Science Centre (Poland).

NATIONAL SCIENCE CENTRE
POLAND

This publication has been peer reviewed by Marko Novak.

ISSN 2191-3250
ISBN 978-3-631-66890-0 (Print)
E-ISBN 978-3-653-06313-4 (E-Book)
E-ISBN 978-3-631-71198-9 (EPUB)
E-ISBN 978-3-631-71199-6 (MOBI)
DOI 10.3726/b15364

Peter Lang – Berlin· Bern · Bruxelles · New York ·
Oxford · Warszawa · Wien

This publication has been peer reviewed.

www.peterlang.com

Preface

This publication was written under the implementation of the research project titled "*The influence of judicial decisions on the discretionary power of public administration in the law application processes*" financed by National Science Centre in Poland. The research had two goals. The first goal was the analysis and description of how and to what extent judgements of administrative courts in Poland impact decisions concerning application of laws issued by bodies of public administration under discretionary powers they are equipped with, i.e. the extent and manner of using such discretionary powers at various stages of the decision-making process (from initiation of procedure, to determination of the facts of the case, validation and interpretation, to qualification), and, in the consequence, the content of final decision. The second research goal was formulation of optimization postulates, referring on the one hand to manner of using by the administration of arguments formulated in substantiation of court orders (referring to particular decision or decisions issued under similar actual condition), and on the other hand to "communication" between courts and bodies of public administration, and the extent of control exercised by them.

The project's fundamental assumption was the thesis on complexity of factors which may to various extents affect decisions of public administration bodies in their application of laws, in particular, decisions made under discretionary powers of such bodies. Such freedom has in this publication a factual dimension, i.e. on the one hand covering all cases in which the legislator intentionally grants discretionary authorities to the administration, and on the other hand all other sources of such freedom, which are not the effect of intentional actions of the legislator (imperfections of legal language, social context of law, etc.). All that comprises a freedom sphere for public administration to the extent of reasoning used in the law application process and content of decisions issued. Content of specific decisions may be affected by variety of legal (legal standards) and other (economical, political, social) factors. The bigger the scope of discretionary powers of public administration, the bigger impact on the whole process and the form of final resolution of other factors than legal ones. Bear in mind, however, that on the one hand public administration is the sort of organization with specific objectives and goals, while on the other hand bodies of public administration are not independent and function within complex organizational and political systems. Thus, specific features of public administration make it (at least potentially) interested in the "content" of decisions issued. It may mean that in some cases legality of actions may be compromised, at the benefit of other criteria (e.g. cost-effectiveness, efficiency, consistency with political goals).

Modern democratic countries fitted out their legal systems with a series of solutions preventing administration from breaching laws, and protecting individuals against arbitrary decisions of public administration, not based (or based in part) on legal standards in force. In this context, control of administrative decisions by independent courts is of special significance. Polish legislative body decided to grant it to specially created courts – administrative courts, with the control criterion being the consistency of decisions issued by administrative bodies with law in force. Control by courts of legality of decisions issued in exercise of administration body of decision-making freedom is not limited, however, to simply stating of consistency or inconsistency of standards included in litigation law and material law in force, but it is confronted with axiology of given division of law and the whole legal system, and even legal order. Therefore, a question arises how and to what extent (how "deep" and how "wide") court orders may affect the extent and the manner of exercising by bodies of public administration of discretionary powers granted to them. Now a hypothesis may be formulated that administrative courts, controlling legality of decisions issued, affect directly or indirectly the decision-making freedom of public administration bodies – restricting it on the one hand, while focusing it on the other hand.

In this context the key problem is with the analysis of adjudication practice and related administrative decisions, in order to provide an answer to question about how courts affect decisions of public administration bodies administration decisions issued in their exercise of decision-making freedom. Analyses performed under the research project covered adjudication of administrative courts, and their goal was to determine the specificity of feedback between administrative courts and bodies of public administration. Answers were sought to the following questions: (1) whether rulings of administrative courts have impact only on resolutions decided in specific case, or lead to adopting by bodies of administration of "decision-making approach" of sorts with regard to cases with similar actual condition, and (2) whether the impact of rulings by administrative courts in cases to which discretionary powers of administrative body apply on other decisions of the same body substantiates the statement on indirect effect of court to the content of administrative decisions; therefore not only departing from legality as the control criterion, but also going beyond the role of court.

Findings from the above-mentioned analyses were compared with legal solutions and practice functioning in legal systems of various European countries. Their critical assessment enabled grasping similarities and differences as compared with the Polish model of court supervision exercised over public administration. All that leads in consequence to the formulation of optimization postulates with regard to possible and acceptable methods of administrative courts affecting the decision-making authority of administration bodies, both to the extent of control ("depth" and "width") and to the extent of interfering with such authority. Observations were also made concerning the use by administration of arguments formulated in substantiation of court orders (referring to particular decision or decisions issued under similar actual condition), and on the "communication" between courts and bodies of public administration.

The original research concept was decision analysis and systemic analysis. Further, due to the fact that in the state governed by laws functioning of public administration bodies is based on legal standards in force, the research covered also the analysis of legacy legislation in, broadly understood, discretionary powers of public administration, its expressions and forms, control measures, as well as the analysis of (procedural and material) laws in force. The main subject of the study will be the ruling of administrative courts. Subject to research was ruling activities by Poland's administrative courts in three periods: 1987–1988, 2000–2001 and 2014–2016. The review of substantiations for rulings from various stages of democracy development (the fall of real socialism, building of stable democracy, and present condition, 10 years into European Union) enables observation of possible changes in courts' approach to freedom of administrative decision-making process, and provides answer to question whether the model of controlling by courts of such freedom underwent significant transformation throughout those years. The project also made use of comparative method, by relating findings from analyses performed to systemic solutions and practice functioning in other European countries.

Deliberations in this publication are the summary of works completed under the research project, and as such they have been presented earlier (at the individual stages of project implementation, orally and in writing[1]) and submitted for critical review of scientific circles in Poland and abroad, which permitted

---

1 Partial findings were published in following documents: A. Szot, *Swoboda decyzyjna w stosowaniu prawa przez administrację publiczną*, Lublin 2016; A. Szot, *Discretionary powers of the public administration in law application processes and its judicial control*, [in:] *Discretionary power of public administration. Its scope and control.*, eds. L. Leszczyński, A. Szot, Frankfurt am Main 2017, pp. 89–103; A. Kalisz, A. Szot, *Modele komunikacyjne w procesach stosowania prawa*, [in:] *Prawo i polityka w sferze publicznej. Perspektywa wewnętrzna*, eds. P. Jabłoński, J. Kaczor, M. Pichlak, Wrocław 2017, pp. 75–86; A. Szot, *The Influence of European Court of Human Rights' Jurisprudence on Public Administration Governance Processes*, [in:] *Global Governance and Its Effect on the State and Law*, ed. Martin Belov, Frankfurt am Main 2016, pp. 229–242.

formulation of final conclusions. If dissertations were published outside the extent permitted by the grant, there is clear reference attached in the footnote.

Findings of the research are presented in five chapters of this publication. Chapter I is dedicated to presentation of the broad context of analyses, i.e. specificity of public administration functioning, factors shaping administration's discretionary authorities and actual or potential factors determining reasoning under the discretionary powers at their disposal, in the context of decision-based model of law application. Chapter II reviews models of control over public administration exercised by courts in various European countries, which, in connection with detailed descriptions of Polish legal solutions, permitted categorization of impacts that court ruling may have on formulation of administrative decisions. This, in turn, was used as the starting point for further deliberations, in chapters III and IV, which present the actual impact of adjudication of courts exercising control over public administration, on the form of individual decisions on law application (micro scale), and shaping decision-making policies and protection of human rights (macro scale). All that permitted formulating, in chapter V, optimization postulates referring the use by public administration of court rulings and "communication" between courts and administration.

This publication would not have seen the light of day without financial support from National Science Centre and substantial comments by professor Leszek Leszczyński, for which I express my thanks. I also want to thank all persons who offered me good advice, support and motivation throughout the implementation of this research project and preparing its final version.

Adam Szot

Contents

Abbreviations

k.p.a.	ustawa z dnia 14 czerwca 1960 r. - Kodeks postępowania administracyjnego (Dz.U.2017.1257 t.j.) [Act of 14 June 1960 – Code of Administrative Procedure]
p.p.s.a	ustawa z dnia 30 sierpnia 2002 r. - Prawo o postępowaniu przed sądami administracyjnymi (Dz.U.2017.1369 t.j.) [Act of 30 August 2002 – Law on proceedings before administrative courts]
CBOSA	Central Database of Judgments of Administrative Courts (orzeczenia.nsa.gov.pl)
CT	Constitutional Tribunal in Poland
ECHR	European Court of Human Rights
SAC	Supreme Administrative Court of Poland
VAC	Voivodeship Administrative Court

Part I. Discretion of the administration in the application and interpretation of the law

1.1 Decision-based approach to law application processes

The application of the law can be perceived as a process initiated and maintained by a competent public authority, whose final effect consists of a binding legal decision. Such an approach corresponds to the decision-based approach[2] adopted in political sciences that were subsequently transferred to legal sciences. One of its basic assumptions is the belief that a part of the reality can be covered and interpreted as decision-making processes or products of such processes, i.e. decisions.[3] Research issues within the decision-based approach are concentrated around the studying of the decision-making situation, conditions and correctness of individual phases of the decision-making situation, location of the decision-making centre, identification and definition of participants' roles in that process, characteristics of a decision, possibilities of its realization in social conditions, indication of actions aimed at its implementation and also the evaluation of its consequences.

Looking at the law application process from the decision-making perspective makes it possible to distinguish its individual stages (phases). The Polish law doctrine assumes with regard to the decision-making process of the courts[4] that it consists of lines of reasoning referring to:

1. the determination of facts of the case;
2. interpretation of the law consisting of the determination of the source of reconstruction of the normative basis for a decision (validation reasoning) and the determination of its content (derivative reasoning);
3. qualification of determined facts from the perspective of the criteria formulated in the normative basis for the decision;

---

2 R. Snyder, H. Bruck and B. Sapin are considered precursors of the decision-based approach.

3 More in: H. Groszyk, A. Korybski, *Podejście decyzyjne w prawoznawstwie (zarys problematyki)*, [in:] *W kręgu historii i współczesności polskiego prawa. Księga jubileuszowa dedykowana Profesorowi Arturowi Korobowiczowi*, ed. W. Witkowski, Lublin 2008, p. 532.

4 More in: J. Wróblewski, *Sądowe stosowanie prawa*, Warszawa 1988, pp. 93–258.

4. determination of legal consequences;
5. the issue of a final decision and its justification,

each of them ending in the making of a separate fragmentary decision.

The general model of law application by public administration bodies does not materially differ from the judicial model presented above. However, it has to be noted that it has one fundamental difference that can be seen in the administrative decision-making process. A detailed analysis of law application by administering entities makes it possible to notice and distinguish an additional phase of that process that chronologically precedes the fundamental reasoning of the decision-making entity or the determination of facts of the case and the interpretation of the law leading to the qualification decision and to the determination of legal consequences. This initial stage of the law application process of the administrative type can be called the pre-decision phase. During that phase, a decision is made to initiate the process aimed at the issue of a unit decision for an external addressee, i.e. the decision to apply the law. Decision making of the judicial type is (depending on detailed preferences of the legislature) particularly based on the principle of the accusatorial procedure and the court has to "await" the submission of an appropriate motion, however, public administration bodies can take action both upon the application and also act *ex officio*.

The occurrence of the pre-decision phase is the most clearly visible with regard to processes initiated by a body itself in connection with the need to execute tasks imposed on it. The legislature frequently entrusts specific tasks (formulated in a general or more detailed manner) to the public administration but does not indicate any ways of their execution. In such a situation, the decision-maker is obliged to choose such a way to act (task execution form) that, in the decision-maker's opinion, will make it possible to attain the predefined goal most completely and most effectively or at least get closer to its attainment. One of the possible types of such action can be the issue of a unit decision to apply the law. If a body comes to such a conclusion in the pre-decision phase (irrespectively of the selection criteria it may use) it will make a decision to initiate the law application process aimed at the issue of such a decision as a result.

Therefore, the pre-decision phase is the moment in which a body decides (the first fragmentary decision in the process) to go to the fundamental reasoning of the law application process in order to issue a binding unit decision. Additionally, one has to remember that a body can, on the one hand, select another form of execution of its task and, in such a situation, the law application process will never be initiated and, on the other hand, even the transition to the decision-making phase of the process does not entail the assumption that the process will end with the issue of a decision to apply the law.

The pre-decision phase will also occur in those cases where the legislature leaves no possibility of choice to the administering entity as regards the commencement of the process and transition to the fundamental reasoning related to the determination of facts and determination of the law, thus limiting its freedom of decision at this stage of the process. In those situations when the body acts on a motion and its submission implies the need to examine a case, this phase will also occur and will entail the reasoning related to the determination of existence of a competence standard authorizing the examination of a case that, in the context of a specific fact (e.g. the appearance of a motion and facts mentioned in it), entails an update to the obligation to examine the case. The difference between the pre-decision phase in this case and the situation in which the legislature does not unambiguously specify the way in which the administration's action should be executed will be visible, in particular, with regard to the scope of the freedom of decision of the entity applying the law.

Therefore, the pre-decision phase will begin at the moment of the occurrence of a decision-making situation, i.e. the fact that implies, objectively or subjectively (in the opinion of the body), the need to commence the process and will end with the making of the decision to commence the law application process or the decision stating the lack of such need. The former decision is constitutive and its making determines the existence of the decision-making process as the statement of the lack of basis for its initiation ends the related considerations of the public administration body while the conclusion that such a need exists starts the entire reasoning process aimed at the formulation of a unit decision.

Additionally, the decision to commence the law application process made in the pre-decision phase is the first unit decision in the entire process; as a result of its making, the body will go to its principal part, i.e. the decision-making phase encompassing all lines of reasoning indicated in the above-mentioned law application model.

From the chronological perspective, this phase precedes the principal decision-making process. Additionally, the meaning of findings established in it for the process justifies the need to perceive it as its immanent part. The separation of the pre-decision phase makes it possible to capture the complexity of processes taking place in certain types of cases of interest to administration bodies prior to the making of the decision to commence the law application process. Depending on the case type, this phase can be very complex or time-consuming or it can be minimized, entailing the almost automatic decision to commence the law application process.

The process of law application of the administrative type consists of two main phases, i.e. the pre-decision phase (pre-jurisdiction) that determines the existence of the case and the decision phase (jurisdiction) determining the content of the final decision. It is also worth noting that the former takes place beyond the procedural regulations regulating the principal administrative procedure, which is material from the perspective of the subsequent control over the law application process. Such regulations mainly include the Code of Administrative Procedures in Poland, hereinafter referred to as the k. p. a[5].. Therefore, the law application process cannot be equated with the formalized administrative procedure. The administrative procedure has to be understood as a sequence of procedural acts regulated under the procedural law, initiated by public administration bodies and other entities in the procedure to settle an individual case in the form of an administrative decision. The law application process is a wider concept; it covers the administrative procedure understood in that manner as well as actions taken before its formal commencement and, as a consequence, determining its existence.

This perspective corresponds to the construction of the "administrative jurisdiction" suggested in the Polish law science and understood as the specification and individuation of the general and abstract legal norm executed by the competent state body.[6] We can discuss the administrative jurisdiction from the dynamic perspective as a set of activities of a body "aimed at the issue of an individual ruling" and from the static perspective as "an administrative act ending the process, containing specified rights or obligation of an individual addressee".[7] In this sense, it mainly refers to material aspects of the law application process, which cannot be equalled with the administrative procedure dependent on procedural standards. As J. Zimmermann writes: "one has to look for the characteristics of the jurisdiction first in material standards and, only after that, in rules of procedure".[8]

The law application process always begins (in essence) before the commencement of the administrative procedure and is primary with regard to that procedure. It is even possible that the process may begin and end without the initiation of the administrative procedure. Additionally, the issue of a substantive decision for an external entity to model its rights or obligation is only

5 The act of 14 June 1960 – Code of administrative Procedures (Dz.U.2017.1257 ct.).
6 J. Zimmermann, *Polska jurysdykcja administracyjna*, Warszawa 1996, p. 5.
7 Ibid.
8 Ibid.

possible in the current legal situation with the execution of the procedure regulated in the Code of Administrative Procedures.

In this sense, the jurisdiction (decision-making) phase of the administrative type of the law application process consists of two parts (stages), i.e. the preparatory one and the principal one. In the preparatory phase, having made the decision to commence the law application process, the body makes arrangements regarding the grounds for the initiation of the formal administrative procedure. The principal phase consists of that very procedure. The form of the preparatory phase can vary depending on the legislature's preferences and the transition to the principal part can depend on the evaluations made by the body or the contents of legal standards in force.

From the material perspective, the law application process consists of a range of fragmentary decisions that eventually lead to the issue of the final decision. Such a decision can have various "names" under the procedural regulations in force (decision, ruling, order, etc.). However, its nature is of key importance rather than the name. A decision is understood as a non-random choice of action[9] – the formulation of a unit standard specifying someone's rights or obligations, determining legal consequences of a legal standard in a specific situation. Therefore, a decision has to be understood as an act of will of a public administration body whose goal is to organize the society, an act of choice between various interests and values that are frequently contradictory for entities, organizations and also between entities and organizations.[10] A decision understood in that manner is an act of application of a standard of the administrative material and procedural law in an outer sphere[11] and goes beyond its definition formulated pursuant to procedural regulations (e.g. the Code of Administrative Procedures).

When analyzing the process of law application by the public administration from the decision-making perspective, one has to observe a few important dependencies. Five categories of the political decision-making analysis are distinguished as a rule: a decision-making situation, decision centre, decision-making process, the decision and the implementation of the decision[12] that can be referred to the study of the law application processes. The decision-making situation occurring in the pre-decision phase and during the process has already been discussed above; the topic will be detailed further in this publication.

9 L. Habuda, *Transformacyjne decyzje i decyzyjne procesy*, Wrocław 2005, p. 26.
10 E. Knosala, *Zarys teorii decyzji w nauce administracji*, Warszawa 2011, pp. 23–29.
11 M. Jaśkowska, *Związanie decyzji administracyjnej ustawą*, Toruń 1998, p. 45.
12 More in: Z. J. Pietraś, *Teoria decyzji politycznych*, Lublin 1990, pp. 27–29.

Topics related to the decision centre, i.e. the administrative body and its operating conditions will also be discussed, also with regard to the final decision and, in particular, the influence that other (earlier) decisions regarding law application (especially court rulings) can have on it. The last two categories of the political decision-making analysis, i.e. the implementation of a decision and the evaluation of its effects that go beyond the classic model of law application are worth discussing here. It is only possible to capture them if one adopts a wider perspective. The *sensu largo* approach to the law application process assumes that the decision-making process ends not at the moment of the adoption of a unit settlement but rather at the moment of the exhaustion of all legal appeal and verification measures, its implementation or forced execution. In this sense, the *sensu stricto* law application decision becomes the beginning and a part of further actions and decisions. For example, if one adopts the perspective of a party (addressee of the decision) or the society (as a whole or its concerned members) it can be concluded that the process will end at the moment of the exhaustion of all the possible (ordinary and extraordinary) means of appeal and execution measures (implementation of the decision or its forced execution). The adoption of such a perspective makes it possible to distinguish "additional", potentially occurring phases of the law application process, i.e. the appeal phase, implementation phase and execution phase. They are a part of the process that has already started and awaits its completion.

However, in the light of the objective of this publication, the perspective of the decision-making entity for which the application of the law ends at the moment of the issue of the final decision is adopted in order to try and answer how court rulings can influence the reasoning of an administration body and the content of the final decision. However, it does not mean that a wider perspective will not be observed in the paper; on the contrary, the body that has completed a case continues to be interested in the subsequent "fate" of the decision it has issued and in whether it will remain valid after a potential appeal or complaint to the court or whether it will be voluntarily executed or it will be necessary to enforce the required behaviour of the addressee. Phases mentioned above (i.e. the control phase and the implementation phase) will be treated as separate processes taking place according to the above-mentioned model of the decision-making process.

1.2 Determinants of the public administration actions

The public administration is the topic of analyses conducted according to varied approaches, perspectives and research theories. Continued attempts at the capturing of that "phenomenon" usually fail and the origins of that failure can be seen in the rapidly changing reality and the need for permanent redefinition of existing concepts, institutions and structures. The public administration is not static, it is subjected to continuous changes and transformations and operates in complex civilizational conditions.[13] Legal sciences have been making attempts to define that phenomenon from two perspectives: the subjective and the objective one (sometimes called functional). The subjective definition of the public administration indicates a system of institutions (bodies) established and given the powers to conduct the organizational and managerial activities of the state.[14] In this context, the public administration is perceived as a specific structure of the state consisting of various entities. The said definitions refer to tasks and functions that the legislature imposes on entities and the public administration thus defined is one of the forms of realization of a function of the state that involves the direct and practical execution of tasks of the state.[15] However, contemporary research of these topics seems to be dominated by trends to combine both perspectives mentioned above and to describe the public administration from the subject-object perspective (object-subject). The administration understood in this manner can be defined as "a set of organizational and executive actions, activities and ventures pursued in the public interest by various entities, bodies and institutions on the basis of a law and in forms specified under the law",[16] as "consisting of people organized for the purpose of the continuous, systematic realization of the common good focused on the future as a public mission involving mainly (but not exclusively) the ongoing execution of laws and, to this end, equipped with the state sovereignty as well as material and technical means"[17] or as "the totality of organizational and executive actions for the realization of the common good by entities (not necessarily state-owned) bound

---

13 See Z. Niewiadomski, *Pojęcie administracji publicznej*, [in:] *System prawa administracyjnego*, vol. 1: *Instytucje prawa administracyjnego*, eds. R. Hauser, Z. Niewiadomski, A. Wróbel, Warszawa 2010, pp. 3–4.

14 See W. Dawidowicz, *Wstęp do nauk prawno-administracyjnych*, Warszawa 1974, p. 12; J. Łętowski, *Prawo administracyjne dla każdego*, Warszawa 1995, pp. 10–11.

15 See M. Jaroszyński, *Przedmiot, zakres i ogólna charakterystyka administracji i prawa administracyjnego w PRL*, [in:] *Polskie prawo administracyjne. Część ogólna*, eds. M. Jaroszyński, M. Zimmermann, W. Brzeziński, Warszawa 1956, p. 28.

16 See H. Izdebski, M. Kulesza, *Administracja publiczna – zagadnienia ogólne*, Warszawa 2004, p. 93.

17 See I. Lipowicz, *Istota administracji*, [in:] *Prawo administracyjne*, ed. Z. Niewiadomski, Warszawa 2002, pp. 27–28.

with the law regulating the basis and forms of its operation, remaining under the social control".[18] The adoption of the subjective-objective outlook on the public administration makes it possible to capture the complexity of its operating conditions. On the one hand, the subjective-objective approach to the public administration refers to the structure of entities established and given the competence to carry out the organization and managerial activity of the state and, on the other hand, it refers to the realization of such competence in the context of tasks imposed on the administration.

The public administration understood in this manner is responsible for the execution of tasks imposed by the legislature. Such tasks include, on the one hand, the activity involving the "simple" fulfilment of duties resulting from the contents of legal standards in force and, on the other hand, creative activity related to the need for an active and effective management of a specific area. It is also stressed that acting for the common good is the guiding principle for public administration bodies in democratic states.

The public administration as a whole and its individual bodies operate in a complex system of connections, e.g. legal, organizational or political. All of them (as well as "impulses" coming from them) can influence administering entities directly or indirectly and, as a consequence, can influence the direction of actions taken and the contents of specific decisions including decisions to apply the law.

Organizational connections in the administration can be analyzed and discussed from the micro or macro perspective. The former relates to a single body that forms a complex organizational structure with its entire back office. Noticing this perspective entails the issue of the efficient internal management that should strive to continuously improve the effectiveness of the operations. The macro perspective highlights the connections and relations between various bodies in the structures of the state administration. As a part of that structure, it is linked to other elements of the structure with legal bonds of double nature. On the one hand, they are relations of the hierarchical subordination and supremacy and, on the other hand, relations based on the distribution of tasks among administering entities in various areas of social life. The occurrence of such relations, depending on their nature (management, coordination, cooperation, control, supervision), entails the possibility of bigger or smaller interference of the bodies with others' actions.

One has to remember that the public administration as a whole as well as its individual bodies were established to perform specific functions and execute

18 Ibid., p. 58.

indicated tasks. Additionally, the legislature equipped it with specific (limited) resources to enable the effective fulfilment of its obligations. The execution of tasks with limited resources necessitates their effective management in a rapidly changing socioeconomic environment. Therefore, the praxeological aspect of activities of the administration becomes increasingly important.[19] It means that decision-making processes and their effects should be optimal in specific conditions. The activities of each administering entity to which the legislature entrusted specific tasks and functions and equipped it with specific "tools" of their realization are more or less accounted for. The assessment takes place as a part of a complex (legally defined) administration control system. A negative evaluation of activities of a body can constitute the basis for a request or order regarding the implementation of various corrective plans. It can also lead to sanctions against a body or specific individuals responsible for the contents and quality of actions taken, in particular, against the office holder. In practice, such interactions directly influence the interest of the administering entity in the direction and contents of the actions taken and, as a consequence, their direction within the limits of the available freedom. Therefore, the activities of administering entities are influenced not only by legal standards but also by internal organizational standards understood as rules of conduct applicable in specific situations, created by an organization or imposed by a competent entity.

The influence of political factors on the activity and decision-making of the public administration can be seen on two levels: politics with regard to the administration and the politics in administration.[20] The former is related to the determination, directly or indirectly, of tasks of the administration. The influence of politics on the determination of goals and functions of the state and its bodies is doubtless and the public administration is the basic apparatus ensuring the execution of public tasks on various levels of public authority.

Political decisions can influence the definition of goals in three ways. Firstly, via the legislative activity when values preferred by the prevailing political option

---

19 J. Łukasiewicz stresses that the effectiveness and efficiency of the authority is its inherent feature. More in: J. Łukasiewicz, *Sprawnościowe przesłanki organizacji i funkcjonowania aparatu państwowego*, [in:] *W kręgu problematyki władzy, państwa i prawa. Księga jubileuszowa w 70-lecie urodzin Profesora Henryka Groszyka*, Lublin 1996, p. 158.

20 J. Boć makes such a distinction, *Pojęcie administracji*, [in:] *Prawo administracyjne*, ed. J. Boć, Wrocław 2010, pp. 18–22. See J. Jeżewski (*Polityka administracyjna. Zagadnienia podstawowe*, [in:] *Administracja publiczna*, eds. A. Błaś, J. Boć, J. Jeżewski, Wrocław 2004, p. 316) who distinguishes "policy towards the administration" and "policy of the administration".

become binding legal standards. Secondly, through the need for administering bodies to refer to the "public interest" category ("common good") in each of its actions, which requires the referral to current goals and objectives of the state every time. Thirdly and finally, their influence can be observed with regard to a specific administrative policy as one of the detailed policies realized as a part of the internal policy of the state with the legislature leaving a certain degree of freedom to the administration as regards the selection of directions or forms of activity. In that case, politics can directly or indirectly influence their determination. The literature notices that the administrative policy is sometimes identified with the public policy.[21]

This area is also linked to another plane of analysis of the influence of politics on decisions made by the administration, i.e. politics in the administration. It is worth to indicate political dependencies of certain bodies whose office holders come from the political appointment or are elected after the nomination by a specific political party. They are responsible for their decisions and also for the decisions of bodies subordinated to them and subjected to the evaluation of entities that nominate them, which are also frequently authorized to dismiss them. In this case, the criterion of the evaluation of actions taken can involve, in particular, the compliance with defined directions of the political activity. In this area, M. Stefaniuk observed accurately that "the degree of politicization of the administration's activity varies in different parts of the administrative apparatus and in different periods".[22]

Additionally, representatives of the doctrine notice the influence of politics on the operation of the public administration and stress that politics has to be understood as a "system of non-legislative and postulative statements of where, when and how to use material and organizational possibilities of the state and the local government"[23] not connecting it to a political line of a specific party. At the same time, one cannot forget that the real influence of ruling political parties on the operation of the public administration is huge.[24]

---

21 More in: M. Kulesza, D. Sześciło, *Polityka administracyjna i zarządzanie publiczne*, Warszawa 2013, pp. 18–19.

22 M. Stefaniuk, *Działanie administracji publicznej w ujęciu nauk administracyjnych*, Lublin 2009, p. 113.

23 J. Boć, *Pojęcie administracji*, op. cit., p. 18.

24 As H. Izdebski rightly emphasizes, the organizational (and even personal) division into the political authority and the administration cannot be introduced fully due to the tradition of combining these two functions in the persons of heads of the administration

Finally and primarily, the operation of the public administration is influenced by the legal standards in force. All actions of the administering entities that can influence rights and obligations of external entities need to have a clear legal basis. The public administration exists to such an extent in which it is established under the law. The law determines its decision-making structure, tasks and forms of their execution as well as the contents of rights and obligations imposed on addressees as a result of the realization of standards of the material administrative law.[25] On the one hand, legal standards define the structure of the administration and its interconnections and, on the other hand, they define its activity areas indicating, in a more or less detailed manner, its tasks as well as ways and forms of their execution. In a state under the rule of law, all actions taken by the public administration need to have a legal basis and be within its limits. In such a state, the legality of operations of the administration is a value that becomes a priority (even at the expense of other values). The law is also an activity model for administering entities. That model determines a directive of specific behaviour, provides a basis for the objectification of the contents of actions, enables the creation of specific, established and repeatable sequences of actions.[26] Therefore, the law is the basic determinant of the degree of freedom available to administering entities. Legal standards can provide for the "binding" of a body (if the statement of an occurrence of a specific fact implies the need for a decision having a specific content) or can make the processes more flexible by leaving to the body the possibility of choice of a direction of action, selection of means to achieve the goal or the eventual shape of the final decision (within limits defined by the laws).

(prime minister, ministers and also executive bodies of local governments) due to the nature of the political function (policy modelling and guarantee of its execution) and the administrative function (creative realization of defined goals). At the same time, he observes that "the public administration should be excluded from the scope of operating principles of the 'petty politics' […], however, it cannot be separated from the *policy* area, where politicians cannot fail to cooperate with expert officials". – H. Izdebski, *Fundamenty współczesnych państw*, Warszawa 2007, pp. 212–213.

25 Z. Niewiadomski, *W poszukiwaniu istoty administracji publicznej*, [in:] *System prawa administracyjnego*, vol. 1: *Instytucje prawa administracyjnego*, eds. R. Hauser, Z. Niewiadomski, A. Wróbel, Warszawa 2010, pp. 40–41.

26 See M. Stefaniuk, *Działanie administracji publicznej w ujęciu nauk administracyjnych*, op. cit., p. 174.

1.3 Position of the administration body in the law application process[27]

Law application of the administrative type is a process initiated by an entity to which the legislature entrusted the execution of public administration tasks. Contrary to the judicial type, both the public authority body and a non-public entity equipped with specific competencies enabling the realization of such tasks can be the decision-makers. These entities are collectively referred to as "administering entities" or "administering bodies". Therefore, the public administration consists of each entity to which the law assigns the administration functions or for which the law creates the bases for the assignment of such a function and the assignment has taken place. To avoid repetitions and ambiguities further in this publication, terms such as the "administering body", "administration body" and the "administering entity", "decision-making entity" or "decision-maker" shall be used interchangeably. At the same time, the entity applying the law is not the addressee of the issued decision in any official or organizational relationship. The decision-maker can imperiously model rights and obligations of the addressee of a decision; however, legal standards in force are the source of that right.

In turn, the organizational subordination is a characteristic feature of the decision-maker of the administrative type. It is a part of a complex apparatus based on hierarchical subordination relations (and the resulting possibility of a direct interference of a body higher in the hierarchy with the activity of a body occupying a lower position) and operating in the system of control and supervision not directly linked to the hierarchical subordination but causing similar effects. The possibility of interference with the activities of a specific administering entity applies to its activity as a whole or its activity in selected areas rather than interference with the contents of a unit decision issued with regard to a citizen (addressee of a decision). The latter cannot occur in a state under the rule of law.

Political factors influence the administering entity. In an extreme case, such influence can manifest as the political dependency of an entity applying the law or a person performing such function. It results from the fact that certain public administration bodies are managed by individuals being political nominees and politically responsible for their actions. The influence of politics is unavoidable – and also justified – in the administrative type irrespectively of its understanding

27 More in: A. Szot, *The Administrative Type of Application of Law*, "Studia Iuridica Lublinensia" vol. XXIV, no. 2 Lublin 2015, pp. 99–114.

and symptoms of influence; however, it is inadmissible when it comes to the application of the law by courts in a state under the rule of law.

Organizational and political relations and, more importantly, the possibility for administration bodies to "account for" their activities determine their direct interest in the contents of an issued decision, including the decision to apply the law. This fact is related to the need to execute tasks entrusted to the body. The body is interested in each of its issued decisions to make it possible for that body to complete its tasks or to get closer to their completion. The effectiveness of activities pursued by public administration bodies is subject to verification in a complex system of relations mentioned before. From that perspective, an entity applying the law is liable for the contents of its decisions to another body that, in the light of its statutory position or competencies granted, performs the supervisory and control function as regards the rational management of resources of the decision-maker and the effective execution of tasks entrusted to it. In addition to the legality of actions, praxeological criteria prevail in the evaluation of decisions issued by a body. Additionally, the political entanglement of certain bodies also results in the evaluation of the contents of decisions issued or their effects from the perspective of compliance with political objectives. In extreme cases, a person performing the function of a body can be removed from office (or bear other consequences) if the evaluation of actions (as a whole, rarely referring to individual decisions) is negative (irrespectively of the adopted evaluation criterion).

It means that, for the body applying the law, each decision-making process is to a degree linked to tasks that the body has to account for. The subject of a unit decision to apply the law consists of the definition of rights or obligations of its addressee; however, the issue of such a decision is, on the one hand, the goal in itself for the body and, on the other hand, also a component of a wider process of management of a specific part of the reality. From this perspective, the body is interested in a single decision fulfilling all the adopted criteria (in particular, the legality and, depending on preferences, also other criteria, e.g. economic effectiveness, compliance with political goals, etc.) and, in this manner, being incorporated in the law application policy within the area directed by that body.

At the same time, the basis for all activities of an entity applying the law in a state under rule of law is in the competence standards decoded from specific standard-creating facts recognized and accepted in a legal system as sources of the law. In the statutory law culture, such facts are usually legal regulations in force, contained in legal acts having an appropriate legal effect. In principle, if the legislature does not permit such a situation the competence given to a body cannot be delegated. Legal standards in force also determine the scope of procedural activities initiated by the administration body in the law application process and the contents of the final decision. Such regulations also offer a specific scope of decision-making freedom to the decision-maker according to the legislature's will. The legislature equips administration bodies with a specific scope of discretionary powers entailing, among other things, the assignment of tasks with no clear determination of the method of their execution, introduction of general reference clauses to a legal text, waiver of the formulation of legal definitions or the formulation of an authorization to make decisions as a part of the administration's discretion. The source of discretionary authority also consists of other factors independent of the legislature's will and related, among other things, to the imperfection of the legal language, specificity of law application processes or the dynamics of social changes, which will be discussed further hereinafter in this work.

Within the limits of the available freedom of decision, there is a range of factors influencing an administration body, with law playing the main role and also constituting their limit. Additionally, organizational and political factors that can supplement each other (intensifying their influence in a way) or mutually limit or even eliminate themselves can also, directly or indirectly, influence the law application process and the content of a specific decision. The influence of the latter two groups of factors is not permitted in the judicial type of law application. This fact leads to decisions being made in the administration in the situation of a potential conflict of interests.[28] Various interests are disclosed and interoperate throughout the entire process, influencing the reasoning of the decision-making entity and, as a consequence, the eventual content of its decision. This is a potential conflict and it does not always materialize.

1.4 Discretionary power of administering entities

Such freedoms can be studied from the dynamic perspective (related to the decision-making process or an ordered sequence of actions) or from the static perspective (covering the analysis of sources of legal standards from the point of view of the scope and type of freedom available to the decision maker).[29] In

---

28 More in: M. Myślińska, A. Szot, *Analiza konfliktowa w administracyjnym typie stosowania prawa (zarys problematyki)*, [in:] *Państwo, prawo, polityka – księga poświęcona pamięci Profesora Henryka Groszyka*, Lublin 2012, pp. 230–241; P. J. Suwaj, *Konflikt interesów w administracji publicznej*, Warszawa 2009, passim; Compare H. Groszyk, A. Korybski, *Konflikt interesów i prawo*, Warszawa 1990, passim.

29 M. Król, *Pojęcie luzu normatywnego stosowania prawa*, „Państwo i Prawo" 1979, no. 6, p. 62.

the light of the objective of this work, i.e. the description and analysis of the influence of judicial rulings on administering entities within the limits of the decision-making freedom available to them and the putting forward of optimization postulates on that basis, both these perspectives will be taken into account further in this discussion. The static analysis of freedoms of decision will take place (to a certain degree of generality) with regard to the search for their sources at different stages of the decision-making process while the dynamic one will try to answer the question about the influence of rulings on the method of "using" freedom granted and to formulate rationalization conclusions on that basis.

The dynamic perspective on decision-making freedoms assumes that the final decision is reached via the gradual elimination and ruling out of abstractly defined alternative choices.[30] The ruling out of consecutive potential choices takes place in stages with the recognition of facts of the case and as their complete determination is being attained.

The entity applying the law starts the process with the general determination of the goal of action and values it will adhere to; after that, it selects one of alternative actions for a given type of cases and, in that manner, goes to the commencement of an action in the light of specific facts. At the first stage, the decision-making entity has a wide range of alternative actions defined by the law in force. With the taking up of consecutive lines of reasoning in the decision-making process, it implements the relativization: first, as regards a given type of cases and, after that, in the context of the facts of the specific case.

It is necessary to indicate here that, in certain types of "standard" and "simple" cases, the body will act "automatically", with no thought given to above-mentioned choices. It will be the case if the body works out specific activity paradigms, with the assumption of the unchanged content of legal standards. Of course, the mechanical nature of actions taken by the administering entity can lead to an error in certain cases. This is why one has to remember that directing attention to any errors in the activity (irrespectively of the sources of such an impulse) will imply the need for above-mentioned lines of reasoning and, after that, their justification in the context of choices made.

From the static perspective, the conducted analyses mainly focus on the degree of freedom "granted to the decision-maker under the legal regulations and standards when making the final law application decision on their basis".[31] However, it should be noted that, in addition to freedoms resulting from the

30 Ibid., p. 63.
31 Ibid., p. 64.

conscious decision of the legislature, other sources of such freedoms also exist (can exist) in decision-making processes. Therefore, the static analysis should take into account not only the degree of freedom vested in the administering entity under legal standards in force. It covers all the situations possible in which the decision-maker will have an alternative choice irrespectively of its source. The grasping of the actual freedom available to the body in law application process requires the indication of the complexity of lines of reasoning initiated at each stage of that process considering both those sources of freedom that emerged as a result of the conscious activity of the legislature and those sources that are inevitably modelled beyond its control.

The theory of the law makes a distinction between "explicit freedoms" and "hidden freedoms". The first group of freedoms is linked to the legislature's deliberate use, in law-making processes, of constructions granting a certain range of freedom to entities applying the law. The second group of freedoms for the body applying the law is a consequence of specific processes of creation and application of the law and the editing of regulations and legal texts and their interpretations.[32]

It is worth noting that "hidden freedoms" can sometimes result from the conscious activity of the legislature that "hides" them purposefully. It is true that this phenomenon is undesirable in a state under the rule of law but it is theoretically possible. E.g. it will be so if the legislature uses a concept in a legal text that has a few similar meanings in the ethnic language and purposefully does not indicate the way to understand it by introducing no legal definition.

For that reason, it is justified to use terms such as "freedoms consciously created" and "freedoms not intended by the legislature/independent of the legislature's will" to distinguish two groups of decision-making freedoms in this publication. It is because the adoption of a language including complements such as "apparent", "hidden" or "latent" precludes a different division of decision-making freedoms, namely those dependent on the legislature's will (and, from that perspective, it is irrelevant whether the legislature disclosed its will to introduce a freedom or concealed it) and those emerging independently of the legislature. It is more important from the perspective of the assumed research objective whether the legislature created a freedom consciously, even if it was concealed, or whether the freedom emerges independently with no interference of the legislature.

---

32 See: S. Wronkowska, *Podstawowe pojęcia prawa i prawoznawstwa*, Poznań 2002, p. 144.

Distinguishing freedoms created consciously and unintended ones is an attempt at their categorization from the perspective of sources of freedom. Freedoms deliberately created by the legislature are components of a specific concept of the law establishment policy implemented with the use of appropriate technical and legal means.[33] Legislative measures modelling the conscious scope of the freedom of decision include: the way in which regulations are formulated and normative acts are constructed (e.g. the use of vague concepts, avoidance of legal definitions, constructing framework legal acts), generation of non-legislative references via which the law system opens to non-legislative criteria and the use of the administrative discretion structure in the administrative law.[34] Sources of decision-making freedoms independent of the legislature's will include: the social context of the law (expressed as a possibility for a decision-making entity to extend the application of a standard to include situations not foreseen by the legislature and in the use of social values), characteristics of the legal language and characteristics of the law application process (resulting from reductionist lines of reasoning taken up in the course of the process or free evaluation of evidence).[35] Therefore, the static analysis of decision-making freedoms has to be conducted considering both groups of sources.

The scope of the decision-making freedom available to the entity applying the law is determined by the contents of legal standards in force; it also results from the specificity and complexity of decision-making processes and the social reality in which such processes take place and in which administering entities operate. This fact authorizes an important thesis: that there are no decision-making processes in which the body applying the law would not have even the minimum degree of freedom.

According to M. Król, the degree of freedom available to the entity applying the law is determined by directives of the choice of action.[36] Her concept defines this rule as comprising the substantive standard and the competence standard

33 L. Leszczyński, *Zagadnienia teorii stosowania praw. Doktryna i tezy orzecznictwa*, Zakamycze 2001, p. 43. As the author indicates: "the legislature does not always has to accept legislative expression in its entirety as the most optimal one; however it has to, at least, agree to the effects of the introduction of constructions creating freedom".

34 Ibid., pp. 43–45.

35 Ibid., pp. 41–43.

36 M. Król, *Pojęcie luzu normatywnego stosowania prawa*, op. cit., p. 64. According to the author, this rule either eliminates freedom of decision completely – it is then the rule determining the contents of decisions, or limits the freedom of decision only and, in such a situation, that rule only directs the choice made by the decision-maker.

as well the directive of the choice of consequences that, to a certain degree (depending on the detailedness of the source), directs the reasoning of the decision-maker. It seems justified to supplement that directive of the choice of action with a procedural standard with regard to the law application processes of the administrative type. It is also worth indicating, as the author herself observes, that not only legal directives of the choice of consequences but also non-legal or paralegal ones occur with regard to the public administration. She notes that "stiff framework of the narrowly defined normative freedom or its limitation with legal directives would be difficult to combine with the operative adaptation of administrative bodies to the changing social conditions and new tasks entrusted to these bodies".[37]

After the adoption of a specific concept of the law system and its sources, it is possible to indicate which directives of the choice of action are legal and which of them are non-legal (paralegal).[38] Depending on the degree to which legally strong rules of the choice of action determine the activity method within the limits of the available freedom of decision, non-legal rules can play varied roles.

In addition to the structure of rules of the choice of action, the way in which final decisions are made within the limits of the available freedom of decision will be influenced by rules of the rational and accurate decision to apply the law.[39] One cannot but agree with this thesis. At the same time, if one applies it to the administrative type of law application it has to be noted, due to numerous non-legal operating conditions of the public administration, that various entities can evaluate the rationality of the contents of issued decisions and the evaluations can vary depending on the adopted point of reference.

Varied terminology is used in the doctrine and in court rulings to denote the scope of freedom available to administering entities when issuing decisions to apply the law: "free discretion", "administrative discretion", "discretionary power", etc. and modifications of these terms.[40] The variability of meaning of such terms depending on the historical moment and the contents of related concepts is also stressed. Additionally, the lack of unambiguous terminology and its inconsistent application can be observed. Depending on the adopted research perspective

---

37 See: M. Król, *Pojęcie luzu normatywnego stosowania prawa*, op. cit., p. 66.

38 Ibid., pp. 66–67.

39 Ibid., pp. 70–72.

40 Compare M. Jaśkowska, Discretionality, *Margin of Decision and Administrative Discretionary Authority – an Attempt at Terminological Clarification* [in:] *Discretionary Power of Public Administration Its Scope and Control*, L. Leszczynski, A. Szot eds., Frankfurt am Main, 2017, pp. 15–36.

or the goal of a justification, they are distinguished and assigned a wider or a narrower meaning or treated as synonyms. This is why the adoption of a consistently used terminology is justified in this work.

The freedom of decision of a public administration body in the law application process is an actual possibility for the administering entity to choose one of the alternative, legally permitted contents of fragmentary decisions in that process that, in its opinion, are supposed to lead to the issue of a final decision most completely attaining the assumed goal in line with the adopted administrative policy within the limits defined by the law in force.

Freedom of decision understood in this manner corresponds to a wide understanding of the concept of the juridical discretionary power that, in principle, can be identified with each manifestation of freedom (of a judge) "irrespectively of whether its origins can be traced back to the statutory authorization or it results from its *praeter* or *contra legem* adoption during the settlement of a unit case that was not exhaustively precise in the law".[41]

A difference between the discretionary authority understood in that manner and the presented approach to the decision-making freedom has to be seen in the fact that, even though sources of the freedom of decision can be non-legal and its "utilization" process can be influenced by non-legal factors, the range of potential variants of choice for the decision-making entity is always limited with the contents of legal standards in force.

However, if we omit that difference it will seem possible to use these concepts interchangeably, provided that we assume that the discretionality of the administration appears in all those cases when the entity applying the law fails to approach the law application process in a strictly formalized and bound manner, and can choose from among at least two legally permitted variants of a solution and the discretionary authority manifests at different stages of that process. Such an approach to the decision-making freedom corresponds to the concept of the discretionary authority, which is used to denote the public administration in the literature written in English.[42] Additionally, it is worth noting that foreign

41 Compare B. Wojciechowski, *Dyskrecjonalność sędziowska – studium teoretycznoprawne*, Toruń 2004, p. 17.

42 See, among others, D. J. Galligan, *Discretionary powers – a Legal Study of Official Discretion*, Oxford 1986, passim; Ch. C. Eriksen, *The European Constitution, Welfare State and Democracy. The Four Freedoms vs National Administrative Discretion*, Routledge 2011, passim; Ch. C. Eriksen, *The Expansion of International Law and the Use of National Administrative Discretion: The Impact on Administrative Battlefields*,

researchers of the topic do not offer such numerous term differentiations as the Polish science.

Two approaches to discretionary authority can be observed in the European law: a narrower one (in principle, identifying such authority with the possibility to choose a settlement) and a wider one (covering freedoms of decision accompanying different stages of law application). However, a wide understanding of the discretionary power that means: "all ways in which the law grants the right to flexibility to the body applying the law, leaving a certain freedom of decision to it, both indeliberately and deliberately" prevails in that law and in CJEU and ECtHR rulings.[43]

An example of the narrow approach to discretionary authority includes the Recommendation of the Committee of Ministers of the Council of Europe of 11.03.1980 concerning the exercise of such power by administrative authorities[44] that defines discretionary authority as a competence giving an administration body a range of freedom with regard to the issued decision, enabling the selection, from among legally permitted decisions, the one that the body considers the most appropriate.[45]

The above-mentioned definition can be interpreted as referring to the reasoning of the entity applying the law at the last stage of the process, i.e. the freedom of settlement formulation. Therefore, it will be identical with the "administrative discretion" term in the meaning used by the domestic doctrine and rulings. It also seems that a different understanding is possible.

If we adopt the decision-making perspective of the law application as the starting point we will observe that the process consists of a range of lines of reasoning, each of them ended with the issue of a decision: a fragmentary decision. Therefore, the definition of the discretionary power introduced in the

New York 2013, passim; G. E. Treves, *Administrative discretion and judicial control*, "The Modern Law Review" 1947, vol. 10, pp. 276–291.

43 More in: M. Jaśkowska, *Uznanie administracyjne a inne formy władzy dyskrecjonalnej administracji publicznej*, [in:] *System prawa administracyjnego*, vol. 1: *Instytucje prawa administracyjnego*, eds. R. Hauser, Z. Niewiadomski, A. Wróbel, Warszawa 2010, pp. 292–298 and rulings referenced there.

44 Recommendation No R (80) 2 of the Committee of Ministers concerning the exercise of discretionary powers by administrative authorities.

45 "The term 'discretionary power' means a power which leaves an administrative authority some degree of latitude as regards the decision to be taken, enabling it to choose from among several legally admissible decisions the one which it finds to be the most appropriate".

above-mentioned Recommendation can be applied to each expression of freedom at all stages of the process and is equivalent to the concept of the decision-making freedom proposed above. The adoption of this reasoning has one doubtless advantage: it expands the scope of provisions of the Recommendation to include all lines of reasoning pursued by administering bodies in the law application process.

It seems permitted in the light of such brief analyses to use terms such as the "decision-making freedom" and "discretionary authority" interchangeably after the adoption of a wide meaning of the latter and after the consideration of conditions indicated above.

Irrespectively of whether the decision-making latitude is intentional or not, the body applying the law cannot choose a fragmentary decision going beyond the legal framework of its operation. Therefore, there is no unbounded freedom of decision or "discretion".[46]

The freedom of decision is an actual freedom, i.e. it covers both freedom in the legal sense and unintentional discretionary powers. The legal existence of the freedom of decision is implied, in particular, by the legislature's purpose principles and technical legal barriers resulting from the imperfection of the legislative technique.[47]

One of the manifestations of the conscious activity of the legislature creating a discretionary power is the use of the administrative discretion structure that the contemporary doctrine and rulings link to the final stage of the law application process, i.e. the moment of determination of legal consequences and, within its limits, the moment of making a choice from among legally permitted possibilities. The administrative discretion and, specifically, freedom of choice available to the administering body within its limits, is one of the manifestations of the freedom of decision.

The freedom of decision refers to all lines of reasoning pursued by the entity applying the law. At the same time, it should be analyzed for each of them separately due to their complexity in individual phases of the process. Therefore, we can talk about the freedom of decision as regards the making of a decision to initiate the law application process, freedom related to the determination of facts and interpretation of the law and, finally, freedom as regards the qualification of facts in the case, determination of consequences of such a qualification and justification of the decision.

---

46 The term of "free discretion" was used in 1980s. More in: Z. Duniewska, *Istota i granice dyskrecjonalnej władzy administracyjnej w świetle standardów europejskich*, „Studia Prawno-Ekonomiczne" 1999, R. LIX , p. 12.

47 Ibid., p. 13.

Part II. Judicial review of administration – models and types of influence

2.1 Models of court control over administration in Europe

Detailed legal solutions in force in European countries with regard to court control over administration differ significantly, which is the consequence of legal, systemic and historical considerations. Nevertheless, it is possible to discuss generalized models in this context. From the viewpoint of comparative legal analyses three matters are of special importance: availability, speed and efficiency of court measures of control over administration.[48] From the perspective of purpose of this publication, the last of them is particularly important, as it refers to the effectiveness of adjudication impact on public administration, and thus on the content of administrative decisions issued. Hence, the issue of the diversity of models of courts impact on bodies of administration, becomes the one of primary importance. The answer is sought to the question whether the impact of court orders on administrative decisions varies depending on court's scope of competence. In this context, matters referring to the structure of courts controlling bodies of administration, and in particular whether that act as separate division of justice system, or as a part of common legal system, or to which degree they belong to executive powers, are of secondary significance.

We can isolate, simplifying a little, two principal models, i.e. one in which substantial resolution of administrative case by a court verifying the administrative decision is permitted and the other, in which it is not permitted (or limited to special occasions). Differences are both in the "depth" of intervention in administrative decisions, and in the possibility to start complementary (or full) decision-making process, in particular as regards facts. In the other case (exclusive or dominant cassatory rights of a court), the adjudication is in principle pursuant to already available material, and evaluation of correctness (in particular lawfulness) of decisions made by the body of administration is assessed (in principle) with reference to actual and legal condition as of the date of decision. In the case of reformatory rights and possibilities for substantial adjudication, it is also possible to consider changes introduced in those two areas following the issuance of decision appealed.

48 See more: D. Popescu, *Judicial Control of Public Administration in European Union Countries*, "AGORA International Journal of Juridical Sciences", no 1 (2013), p. 148.

More in-depth analysis of legal solutions and practice of individual countries indicate however that categorization in three models of court control over administration is justified:[49]

1. model with sole (or dominant) cassatory authorities;
2. model with dominant substantial adjudication;
3. mixed-model, in which, despite reformatory rights of courts controlling administrative decisions, substantial rulings substituting administrative decisions are taken to a limited extent.

The former of indicated models is in force in countries whose legal systems permitted only (or mostly) the possibility of removing from legal circulation administrative decisions inconsistent with verification criteria adopted by such system. Determining such inconsistency by court results in repeal of the decision without substituting it with any substantial solution. In some legal systems exceptions from the rule were introduced, by granting courts with competence to final (substantial) resolution of administrative case or issuing a ruling, in which the subject body shall find the manner of resolving the subject case.[50]

This model is present i.a. in the United Kingdom, where (without going into the structure and systemic positioning of bodies responsible for verification of administrative decisions, i.e. tribunals and courts[51]) it is a court that is solely competent for remedying defective decision of a body. It shall analyze whether decision was made in-line with legal scope of responsibilities of the body of public administration and whether it meets normative standards of just and reasonable decision.[52] Pursuant to legal deeds in force in the United Kingdom, and in particular pursuant to *Civil Procedure Rules 1998, a* demand for court control over administration means verification of the legality of an act of law issued by body of administration.[53] Determination of defects in

49 This categorization was postulated by W. Piątek and A. Skoczylas *Model polskiej jurysdykcji administracyjnej* [in:] *System prawa administracyjnego, vol. 10: Sądowa kontrola administracji publicznej*, R. Hauser, Z. Niewiadomski, A. Wróbel eds., Warszawa 2010, pp. 59–67.

50 W. Piątek i A. Skoczylas, *Model polskiej jurysdykcji administracyjnej* [in:] *System prawa administracyjnego, vol. 10: Sądowa kontrola administracji publicznej*, R. Hauser, Z. Niewiadomski, A. Wróbel, eds. Warszawa 2010, p. 61.

51 See disputes in Anglo-Saxon doctrine referring to systemic position of administrative tribunals. More in: E. Jacobs, *Tribunal Practice and Procedure*, London 2011; C. Harlow, R. Rowlings, *Law and administration*, New York 2009, pp. 486–527.

52 *Regina v Somerset County Council ex parte Fewings and others*, [1995] 1 All Er 513.

53 Civil Procedure Rules 1998, Rule 54.1.

decision results in repeal of such decision and handing the matter over to repeated substantial consideration by the body. Hence, a court may not substitute such decision with a ruling, unless the court decides that returning the case for re-examination is pointless, since there is only one lawful way of proceeding with the case, and circumstances of the case indicate that such decision is the only one that can be made.[54] While analyzing the matter, it is to be pointed out that the right to issue substantial resolutions in the administrative decision verification proceedings is granted to quasi-court administrative tribunals[55] while appealed resolutions may be verified based on diverse evaluation criteria.[56] Due to the purpose of this publication, this problem shall not be further discussed.

Strong cassatory adjudication model of administrative courts is also typical of Hungary's legal system. According to Article XXVIII paragraph 7 of the Chapter of the Hungarian Fundamental Law (Hungarian Constitution): *"Everyone shall have the right to seek legal remedy against any court, authority or other administrative decision which violates his or her rights or legitimate interests."* This provision provides the constitutional foundation of the judicial review of administrative action in Hungary.[57] The fundamental and exclusive criterion of verification by court of administrative decisions is consistency with laws. When exercising control over administration, a court is not entitled to substitute administrative decision with court order. Further, the borderline between legality and substantiation of the decision is not always easy to grasp in Hungarian legislation. For instance it may be difficult to distinguish legality (rationality and reasonableness) and expediency.[58] In particular, court may not interfere with freedom of administrative decisions established by provisions of law in force. Court jurisdiction

---

54 Civil Procedure Rules 1998, Rule 54.19.

55 P. Cane, *Administrative Tribunals and Adjudication*, Portland 2009, pp. 3–6, 69–72.

56 See more: I. Turner, *Judicial Review, Irrationality and the Review of Merits*, [in:] "The Nottingham Law Journal", 15 (2), p. 37; A. Freckelton, *The Concept of Deference in Substantive Review of Administrative Decisions in Four Common Law Countries*, Vancouver 2013, pp. 97–140.

57 A. Kovacs, M. Varju, *Hungary: The Europeanization of Judicial Review*, [in:] "European Public Law", vol. 20 (2014), p. 197. See also Emese Pál, *Towards An Autonomous Administrative Judicial Power?*, "Studia Iuridica Cassoviensia", 5 (2017), pp. 34–46.

58 A. Kovasc, M. Varju, *The Impossibility of Being a National and a European Judge at the Same Time: Doctrinal Rifts Between Hungarian and the EU Administrative Law*, [in:] *Central European Judges Under the European Influence: The Transformative Power of the EU Revisited (EU Law in the Member States)*, ed. M. Bobek, Portland 2015, pp. 197–223.

will be limited in those cases to examine whether the decision is logical and reasonable (apart from other assessment criteria used in any "typical" case).

In legal systems of countries that implemented this model of court control over administration, solutions apply that in many occasions grant courts the right to formulate orders for bodies of administration to issue decisions and to formulate binding guidelines concerning the content of such decisions. Such a solution is present in i.a. Polish legal system, which shall be discussed later in the publication.

"In some cases it may be considered that consequences of such solutions are in fact very similar to the substantial adjudication model.[59] Germany is the example of such a model. In Article 19, German Constitution[60] introduces the general principle: *"Should any person's rights be violated by public authority, he may have recourse to the courts. (…)"*. Further, the concept of "breached law" is understood in this context not only as breached fundamental laws (*Grundrechte*), but also broadly understood rights of individuals. Such laws do not necessarily have to be constitutional or statutory in nature, and they may also be derived from legal activities.[61] The nature of court orders in cases in "general administration proceedings" area depends on the "type" of complaint, and when verifying the administrative decision a court may issue a ruling containing resolution with regard to granting a benefit, may consider the legal relationship as existent or non-existent, or to obligate a body to issue administrative deed (e.g. in case of administration not taking position) or complete the case pursuant to court's legal opinion.[62] In this context we have to point out that German legislator allowed for the possibility of substantial adjudication by courts.[63] The matter of availability of substantial adjudication by administrative courts and its consistency with the constitution generally does not raise any concerns in German legal circles. At the same time there are three forms of judicial deference to agency actions: agency discretion (*Ermessensspielräume*), legislative authorization to the agency to

59 W. Piątek i A. Skoczylas, *Model polskiej jurysdykcji administracyjnej* [in:] *System prawa administracyjnego, vol. 10: Sądowa kontrola administracji publicznej*, eds. R. Hauser, Z. Niewiadomski, A. Wróbel, Warszawa 2010, p. 63.

60 Grundgesetz für die Bundesrepublik Deutschland.

61 M. Sachs, *Grundgesetz*, München 2009, p. 786.

62 W. Piątek i A. Skoczylas, *Model polskiej jurysdykcji administracyjnej* [in:] *System prawa administracyjnego, vol. 10: Sądowa kontrola administracji publicznej*, eds. R. Hauser, Z. Niewiadomski, A. Wróbel, Warszawa 2010, p. 63.

63 Act Verwaltungsgerichtsordnung, BGBl. 1960.

interpret rules (*Beurteilungsermächtigungen*), and the freedom of planning (*planerische Gestaltungsfreiheit*).[64] In every of them court control is limited.

Administrative courts in Austria are also an interesting example as they have recently undergone a transformation from cassatory model to substantial adjudication by courts. The first model existed in Austria by the end of 2013, when Administrative Tribunal[65] (*Verwaltungsgerichtshof) had solely cassatory* rights towards an appealed administrative decision, with sole remedies being repeal or determination of invalidity. Excluded from this area was adjudication in matters of administrative inactivity, where the decision could be substituted for court order.[66] In the consequence of later changes in legislation, in 2014, Austria has two-instance administrative judicature. Pursuant to Article 130.1 *Verwaltungsgerichtsbarkeits-Novelle 2012*[67] courts of the first instance adjudicate in cases of complaints: for inconsistency of administrative decisions with laws, exercise of administrative enforcement measures, inactivity of the body. Further, novelized provisions (Article 130.4) granted courts the right to substantiated (not only cassatory) adjudication in penal administrative proceedings, and in other proceedings, should the actual condition raise doubts, or should determination of specific facts by administrative court be in the best interest of swift and/or cost-effective completion of proceedings. Further, substantial adjudication by first-instance court became a rule of thumb.[68] As regards complaints concerning breach by the administration body of obligation to issue decision, a court, when considering the complaint as substantiated, first focuses on legal matters with general significance and issues the preliminary rulings, charging the body of

64 See more: J. Oster, *The Scope of Judicial Review in the German and U.S. Administrative Legal System*, "German Law Journal", 9 (2008), pp. 1267–96.

65 As in the case of the United Kingdom, we also omit the matter of functioning and decision-making of *quasi-court* bodies, such as independent administrative senates (*UnabhängigeVerwaltungssenate in der Ländern*).

66 J. Łętowski, *Austria* [in:] *Sądownictwo administracyjne w Europie Zachodniej*, ed. L. Garlicki, Warszawa 1990, pp. 164–170.

67 Bundesgesetz, mit dem das Bundes-Verfassungsgesetz, das Finanz-Verfassungsgesetz 1948, das Finanzstrafgesetz, das Bundesgesetz, mit dem das Invalideneinstellungsgesetz 1969 geändert wird, das Bundessozialamtsgesetz, das Umweltverträglichkeitsprüfungs gesetz 2000, das Bundesgesetzblattgesetz, das Verwaltungsgerichtshofgesetz 1985 und das Verfassungsgerichtshofgesetz 1953 geändert und einige Bundesverfassungsgesetze und in einfachen Bundesgesetzen enthaltene Verfassungsbestimmungen aufgehoben werden.

68 R. Winkler, *Vorrang der reformatorischen Sachentscheidung - VwGH 26.6.2014, Ro 2014/03/0063*, ZVG 5 (2014), p. 437.

administration with the obligation to make decision within prescribed time of maximum eight weeks, considering the legal opinion expressed.[69] Administrative Tribunal became the court of the second instance, investigating i.a. appeals to administrative court orders for inconsistency with law. In the event of considering the complaint as justified, it may decide on repealing the appealed order by the court of first instance, or decide with regard to the case substance. Substantial adjudication is possible if the Tribunal is ready to make decision, and decision in the case is in the interest of simplification, facilitation and cost-effectiveness.

The substantial adjudication model of administrative courts is also present in France, where courts are entitled to issue a ruling substituting, in part or in full, an administrative decision in variety of cases. This is the natural consequence of the fact that administrative courts in this country were always considered the part of administration – only not "active administration".[70] Citizens can challenge the lawfulness of administrative decision through various remedies – "the remedy for abuse of power", namely an action for annulment (*recours pour exces de pouvoir*) and – "the remedy of full jurisdiction" (*recours de plein juridiction*), the plaintiff who has suffered from the administrative act can demand pecuniary compensation in administrative courts.[71] On the basis of the powers recognized to the court when considering the merits of the claim one can identify four types of litigation: actions brought on grounds of *ultra vire*s, in which the court may only annul the challenged decision; full litigation or full jurisdiction litigation, in which the judge can reform the administrative act; litigation on interpretation or validity, through a referral for a preliminary ruling made the judicial court to the administrative court, in which the latter rules on the lawfulness of an act without settling the dispute between the parties; and enforcement litigation, in which the court can order a citizen to repair the damage caused to the public domain.[72]

Courts in Serbia, where there are two types of disputes in front of the administrative court, have cassatory and reformatory rights. One is the so-called dispute with limited jurisdiction in which the court is confined to access the legality

69 D. Gut, *Model postępowania sądowoadministracyjnego w Austrii*, „Młody Jurysta", 2 (2017), p. 10.

70 See H. Izdebski, *Francja*, [in:] *Sądownictwo administracyjne w Europie Zachodniej*, ed. L. Garlicki, Warszawa 1990, p. 78.

71 See Z. B. Buğuçam, *Common Principles of Judicial Review of Administration in Europe: A Comparative Study of France, the UK, The ECHT and the EU*, "Law & Justice Review", Year: III, Issue: 5, December 2012, p. 78.

72 H. Flavier, Ch. Froger, *Administrative Justice in France. Between singularity and classicism*, "Brics Law Journal", vol. III 2 (2016), p. 95.

of the administrative act and to annul it entirely or partially and the second one is "dispute with full jurisdiction" in which the court can decide on the administrative case.[73] According to article 42 of Serbian Law On Administrative Disputes "*If the court finds that the challenged administrative act must be annulled, if the nature of the matter so allows and if the facts of the case give a reliable foundation for so doing, it may decide the administrative matter by a judgment. This judgment shall completely replace the annulled act.*"

In Spain the judge can annul administrative decision and, at the same time, can grant "the recognition of an individualized legal situation and the adoption of the suitable measures for its full re-establishment, and among other things, compensation for damages".[74] According to article 106.1 of Spanish Constitution courts control the regulatory power and the legality of administrative acts as well as its compliance with the objectives which justify it.[75]

Finland, where despite generally reformatory competences of administration courts, such decisions are made cautiously, is the example of mixed-model. It means that despite having right to alter the appealed decision, they do not do it, for variety of reasons. For example Finnish Supreme Administrative Court does not exercise its reformatory competence so that, when it quashes a decision denying an administrative permit (such as a building permit or a business permit) as illegal, it would at the same time grant the permit as sought. Instead, the case is remanded to the appropriate permit authority.[76] However this competence is not absolute because administrative courts have only cassatory competence in cases where the administrative authority whose decision is being appealed has an autonomous status external to the state administration; this applies e.g. to municipal authorities. In such cases, when the court upholds an appeal, it can but quash the decision on appeal.[77]

---

73 See more: Dejan Vučetić, *Serbian Judicial Review of Administrative Acts and European Standards for Admininistrative Disputes*, "Facta Universitatis Series: Law and Politics", vol. 3, 1 (2005), pp. 73–90.

74 *Administrative Justice In Europe – Report For Spain* (www.aca-europe.eu/en/eurtour/i/countries/spain/spain_en.pdf) *access: 20.12.2017.*

75 See more: R. J. Sánchez, *The Administrative Justice in Spain: Current Situation And Challenges*, "Brics Law Journal", vol. III 2 (2016), p. 116.

76 Finnish report for the IASAJ Congress in Sydney, March 2010, https://www.aihja.org/images/users/1/files/finland.en.0.pdf, pp. 10–11, access: 10.12.2017.

77 Finnish report for the IASAJ Congress in Sydney, March 2010, https://www.aihja.org/images/users/1/files/finland.en.0.pdf, pp. 10–11, access: 10.12.2017.

According to article 3.2 of Lithuanian act on administrative proceedings[78] the court does not evaluate, whether the disputed act (administrative decision) is economically or politically purposeful, but only determines, whether in a particular case the law was not breached, whether the body of public administration did not exceed it jurisdiction, also, whether a legal act does not contradict purposes, for which the body was established. Upon hearing the case (article 88), the administrative court can: (1) revoke the contested administrative act (part thereof) or obligate the appropriate entity of administration to remedy the committed violation or carry out other orders of the court; (2) oblige the appropriate entity of municipal administration to implement the law, a Government resolution or another legal act; (3) settle the dispute in any other manner provided for by law; (4) award damages or redress of a moral wrong caused to a natural person or an organization by the unlawful acts or omission in the sphere of public administration performed by State or municipal institutions, agencies, services and their employees in the discharge of their official functions (extracontractual liability). Administrative decision may be annulled (article 89) if it is: 1) illegal in essence, i.e., conflicting by its contents with legal acts of superior power; 2) illegal by reason of being adopted by an entity of administration acting outside the remit of his competence; 3) illegal as it was adopted in violation of the basic procedures, especially the rules which were to ensure objective evaluation of all circumstances and validity of the decision; 4) on other grounds recognized as material by the administrative court.

As evidenced by examples above, detailed legal solutions adopted in the area of court control over administration differ significantly by country. Nevertheless, their generalized analysis enables grasping some correlations, which were used as the base for categorization of impacts of adjudication to decision-making processes of administration bodies, which shall be further discussed in Part 2.3 of this publication. This shall be preceded with more in-depth analysis of Polish model, to be used as the axis for any further discussions.

2.2 Model and scope of judicial review of administration in Poland

Due to the fact that public administration bodies are appointed to fulfil more or less specific state functions, review of their actions, including the review of

78 Lietuvos Respublikos administracinių bylų teisenos įstatymas 1999 m. sausio 14 d. no. VIII–1029.

administrative decisions, should be performed according to diversified criteria (relevant for the aspect of society controlled by public authorities). In this context, beside legitimacy of public authority actions, including lawfulness of administrative decisions, the review may also encompass their effectiveness, sound management, purpose, compliance with a given policy line etc. Also, this review system is diversified due to the variety of entities having different reviewing powers. In most general terms, they can be divided into "in-house" administration entities (internal administrative review) and external entities (administrative courts and other bodies duly empowered by their employer, e.g. prosecutor). Detailed structure and functioning of the system of reviewing actions of public authorities have been set out in the existing laws. It should also be noted that, depending on specific solutions, more or less formalized and direct reviewing powers may be held by society as such, or by entities representing its interests or interests of specific groups (e.g. social organizations).

Thus diversified system of reviewing public authority actions is necessary, considering issues dealt with by public administration, and due to its organizational and political relationships mentioned in the introductory paragraphs. Due to the fact that public administration bodies are directly interested in the content of their decisions, including administrative decisions, it is necessary to ensure proper protection of civil rights and freedoms against arbitrariness of these activities.

Administrative review, consisting in investigation whether actions of an authority comply with the stipulated (required by law) status quo and in formulating conclusions in case of any departures, is necessary to ensure proper public authority actions.[79] Administrative court review is believed to be the most significant form of administration review. It is strictly related with the concept of democracy whose canons include judicial protection of public rights and public interests, as well as judicial protection of the objective legal order by construing to that end the right to a fair trial. It is an objective and professional review performed by an independent court, in accordance with a formal procedure, giving full procedural guarantees to parties of a legal relationship.[80]

79 See: J. Zimmermann, *Prawo administracyjne*, Zakamycze 2005, p. 485. According to Zimmermann, review is an integral part of the administrative process and it should be designed to minimize any pathological phenomena in the administrative process, and to be preventive.

80 Ibid., pp. 485–486.

Judicial review of administrative decisions is intended to protect specific values in the legal order, including human rights and freedoms, against illegal activities of public authorities. Polish administrative courts review performance of public administration bodies in terms of their compliance with relevant laws. At the same time, it should be emphasized that administrative courts are entitled to file cassation appeals against administrative decisions and they do not examine the facts of an administrative case.[81] Therefore, during judicial proceedings, arguments related to legitimacy or purpose cannot be taken into account. Only lawfulness of an administrative act is examined, that is correctness of applying legal provisions to the existing facts of a case, accuracy of interpretation and relevance of the adopted procedure concluded with adoption of the contested act.[82] Administrative court is only to determine whether the purposes of court proceedings gathered during an administrative procedure comply with requirements of the existing laws. If the conclusion is negative for the authority, the court will be entitled and at the same time obliged to reverse the settlement appealed against and, e.g. determine to what extent purposes of the proceedings are not relevant for the status quo and therefore, how and to what extent it should be complemented.[83]

In Poland, ruling on lawfulness of administrative acts was entrusted to a separate branch of the judiciary, i.e. to administrative courts, which deliver rulings in two instances. Appeals against administrative decisions are first examined by voivodeship administrative courts (VAC), whereas cassation appeals may be filed to Supreme Administrative Court (SAC). At the same time, powers of administrative courts were limited to issuing cassation (reversal) rulings only. In other words, flaws found in an administrative decision oblige the court to reverse it. At the same time, with a few exceptions discussed in the following section hereof, the court has no right to deliver a ruling interfering in the substance of the decision or replacing this decision.

The Polish model of judicial review of public administration performance is in particular characterized by the following features:

---

81 Pursuant to the ruling of the VAC in Warsaw of 23.11.2011 (V SA/Wa 1654/11), CBOSA: "The court following the appeal against the act (decision, order) or activity, and due to inaction of the public administration body shall not take up the administrative case for final settlement; it only has to review and evaluate performance of this body. It cannot therefore – as a rule – act in place of a public authority and settle the case as regards the substance."

82 See ruling of the VAC in Opole of 19.07.2011, II SA/Op 244/11, CBOSA.

83 See ruling of the VAC in Warsaw of 18.05.2011, II FSK 87/10, CBOSA.

1) administration of justice is done by reviewing actions of public administration bodies in terms of their compliance with relevant laws;
2) jurisdiction of administrative courts is stipulated in the form of a general clause restricted with an exemption clause (competences of Polish administrative courts apply to the majority of public administration activities regarding individual cases, except for cases exempted from this scope);
3) courts act at the request of a competent entity having the capacity to file complaints, which means that the Polish administrative judiciary system is based on public rights protection;
4) autonomy of common courts, including cancellation of the jurisdiction of the Supreme Court over administrative courts;
5) administrative proceedings in two instances;
6) cassation-like nature of rulings issued by administrative courts.[84]

Judicial review of public administration actions, limited to investigation of their legality, also involves examination of the actions in terms of their compliance with procedures stipulated in the legal provisions, identification and indication of any possible discrepancies and their causes, as well as formulating conclusions and recommendations aimed at their elimination. Therefore, review of legality involves checking whether public administration actions are in accord with the existing laws, which means protection of substantive law. In the event administrative court finds a breach of this law, the review will effect in application of measures prescribed by the law, e.g. reversal of the decision appealed against, reversal of a supervision act or obliging an administrative body to issue a decision within a specified time. Therefore, review of public administration performance includes: examining redefinition of the rules of procedure providing grounds for evaluation of the actual fact-finding by an administration authority, required by law; reviewing the method of legal qualification of these facts, which applies to substantive and legal grounds for an administrative decision, including the review of legal interpretation performed by the body; in view of provisions of procedural acts stipulating legal requirements regarding reasoning of an administrative decision (order), reviewing the specific manner of determining actual and legal grounds for the decision in a given case.[85] Predominantly however, protection of substantive rights is linked to protection of subjective rights of citizens which are stipulated in the laws but were violated due to illegal activities of public

---

84 More in: J. P. Tarno, E. Frankiewicz, M. Sieniuć, M. Szewczyk, J. Wyporksa, *Sądowa kontrola administracji*, Warszawa 2006, pp. 20–21.

85 See ruling of the SAC in Warsaw of 25.11.2014, II GSK 1684/13, CBOSA.

administration bodies.[86] Protection of these rights is the primary purpose of establishing an institution reviewing lawfulness of administrative performance, in particular in the form of an administrative decision. And the review from the point of view of lawfulness of the contested act should be understood as evaluation of proper application of legal provisions and accuracy of interpretation.[87]

Administrative court, being the court of cassation, takes no evidence during the proceedings, it does not search for new evidence or new circumstances, but at most explains any doubts as regards charges found in the complaint. Judicial review of administrative decisions is limited to appraisal of the decision-making process and substance of the decision in terms of its compliance with the relevant law and, as a rule, excludes independent determination of the facts of the case by administrative courts. For the same reason, the court reviews the contested decision and the decision-making process to determine whether it involved the specified fault.[88] For public administration review exercised by administrative courts involves investigation whether a public administration body infringed on legal provisions to the extent affecting the outcome of the case. Such review should always take into account the substantive, procedural and competence contexts.[89]

At the same time, J. Zimmermann points out that the lawfulness and purpose criteria may be merged in a judicial review of administrative decisions. He provides an example of a position found in rulings of the Supreme Administrative Court, which in the context of supervision over local authority, is referred to as 'licit purpose' idea. It requires an administrative court not only to examine compliance of the act with a specific rule or set of rules, but also compliance with the purpose for which this rule was established.[90] Irrespective of that, other criteria including purpose may be analyzed by the court in reference to decisions based on administrative discretion, which shall be discussed further in the text.

The court re-examines the administrative decision and the process of determining its final substance. For it should be borne in mind that the subject matter of administrative court proceedings is not only the contested administrative act, but also the operations and activities exercised by an administrative body in the case concluded with this act. Administrative court competences determined

86 See ruling of the VAC in Kraków of 20.04.2012, II SA/Kr 214/12, CBOSA.
87 See ruling of the VAC in Warsaw of 5.04.2010, VIII SA/Wa 268/10, CBOSA.
88 J. Borkowski, *Decyzja administracyjna*, Łódź–Zielona Góra 1998, pp. 163–164.
89 See ruling of the SAC of 7.10.2010, II FSK 870/09, CBOSA.
90 See: J. Zimmermann, *Prawo…* op. cit., p. 474.

above impose an obligation on the judicial authority to appraise the entire course of the administrative procedure in a given case, all transactions and acts issued in the proceedings, including appraisal of the contested decision and delivery of a ruling producing a situation in which no illegal acts or transactions of public administration bodies exist or function.[91] In view of the law application process resulting in an administrative decision, from the point of view of the decision-making analysis (discussed in the first section hereof), reasoning of an administration body subject to judicial review should be presented.

Despite absence of the capacity to determine facts of an administrative case, it should be noted that since the scope and very often method of analyzing the facts of a case is determined in procedural provisions or acts of the substantive administrative law, this aspect of the decision-making process is subject to judicial review in terms of correctness of the findings and their compliance with these rules. The court is obliged to examine whether facts of a case were established correctly, whereas the facts of a case are appraised in accordance with specific provision of substantive law.[92] Judicial review of the correctness of establishing the facts of a case is conducted by analyzing the administrative decision, in particular the part of its reasoning referring to this aspect of the decision-making process and indirectly, by analyzing the facts of a case.

In rulings of the Supreme Administrative Court (SAC)[93] a view has been adopted that limits of administrative court review are determined by limits of an administrative case including the parties and issue examined in the case. This means that during determining the subject matter of the case, exactly those components should be considered, which in reference to the parties of the case is expressed in identity of a party having rights or obligations, whereas as regards the subject matter of the case, in the substance of these rights and obligations, and their legal or factual basis. The scope of judicial review is therefore determined by the subject matter of a given administrative case, determined by legal basis of the delivered ruling. It is the rules of substantive and procedural law that will determine the scope of judicial review of administrative decisions. The aim of this review is not to re-examine the established facts of a case, but to check whether they were correctly established by an administrative entity.

As regards the scope of reviewing the process of establishing the facts of a case in administrative court proceedings, a number of areas analyzed during

91 Compare ruling of the SAC in Warsaw of 20.01.2010, I GSK982/08, CBOSA.

92 See ruling of the SAC of 1.09.2009, I OSK 8/09, CBOSA.

93 See, among others, ruling of the SAC of 21.09.2012, I GSK 40/12, CBOSA;

the proceedings should be distinguished. Firstly, a question should be answered whether the administrative entity correctly appraised the facts leading to initiation of administrative proceedings. As indicated above, public administration body initiates the decision-making process the moment proper circumstances appear. However, pure emergence of the circumstances and launching of the decision-making process does not necessarily imply this process to turn into a formal administrative procedure and end with a substantive decision. As regards proceedings initiated at the request of a party, legal provisions stipulate the requirements to be met by the application and the applicant. The authority must evaluate whether or not the request filed by a given entity can be classified as an administrative case. In this manner, it appraises whether it is competent to deal with the case and whether this entity has a legal interest in the issued decision. Establishment of facts determining the above arrangements and of the method of their evaluation is appraised by the administrative court, both in relation to decisions to refuse institution of the proceedings, as well as to proceedings terminated with an administrative decision.

In proceedings instituted *ex officio*, administrative authority's powers to decide about institution of administrative proceedings will be of different scope, depending on the source providing information about initiation of the decision-making process. Therefore, the scope of judicial review of decisions made by the authority will also vary. For in some cases, the decision-making entity will be obliged to institute formal administrative proceedings in the light of information it receives. In other, the administrative authority shall be free to decide whether or not to conduct administrative proceedings. This group of cases may include decisions made in relation to implementation of tasks, when the authority performs initial appraisal of the social situation in the context of the set goals. Then it is the results of the appraisal that exclusively determine whether in light of the facts, the authority will find it necessary to conduct specific proceedings and issue an administrative decision. The appraisal conducted by the administrative authority in this respect is outside the scope of the administrative court review. For if a legal rule sets out specific tasks for the authorities, then their competences include assessment whether the specific actions are valid. This appraisal is fully verified in the course of administrative proceedings, however due to fact that the rule does not impose the obligation to initiate the proceedings but leaves it for the appraisal of the authority, any decision made by the authority will be legal. It should be stressed however, that such cases do not exclude judicial review of the correctness of the fact-finding process.

It is exactly the correctness of the fact-finding process which is the second aspect subject to administrative court review. The review is conducted in line with two approaches – procedural and substantive. In the first approach, the court examines whether an administration body pursued the proceedings to take evidence in a proper manner. The review is specifically oriented if legal rules impose an obligation on the authority to take specific evidence. In such situations, judicial review of the correctness of the fact-finding process involves determination whether the authority actually took this evidence in the course of administrative proceedings. This does not mean however the exclusion of other aspects of the fact-finding process from the review of the administrative court in such cases. Just like in other instances (when no legal rule imposes an obligation to take specific evidence on the authority), actions of the decision-making entity are subject to comprehensive review of the administrative court in the context of implementation of the previously discussed general principles of establishing the facts of a case. In both cases, the review according to the procedural approach must be complemented with a substantive review, as the purpose of the proceedings to take evidence is to ascertain an objective truth, and not only unreflectively take all evidence required by law. In light of the above, it should be concluded that an administration body is free to take any evidence, besides the evidence which it is obliged to take by the valid rules, intended to establish the facts of a case and consequently, to issue an administrative decision. Administrative court will review whether an administration body, based on evidence taken, established a sufficient number of facts of a case to issue an optimized administrative decision.

While evaluating the correctness of the fact-finding process according to the substantive approach, the court will examine the following issues:

- whether facts of a case were established to a sufficient extent – the court will evaluate completeness of analyses intended to establish the number of facts that allows to issue an administrative decision;
- whether evidence was taken correctly – according to the procedural approach, the court only appraises whether the administration body took all evidence required by law or necessary to establish the facts of a case, whereas according to the substantive approach, the court will focus on the correctness of taking the evidence and on correct appraisal of the force of specific evidence;
- whether the facts were appraised properly (in case of facts determined in the legal rules in an evaluative manner) – if the legislator prescribed the need to value specific facts, the evaluation should be performed by the law administration body but is subject to judicial review;

It should be noted however, that the scope of reviewing the correctness of the fact-finding process, both in relation to the facts initiating the proceedings and facts determining the substance of an administrative decision, will depend on specific facts of the case, in conjunction with validation and interpretation findings.

Due to the fact that administrative court examines lawfulness of the decision-making process and substance of the administrative decision, it may be assumed that the scope of establishing the facts of a case is the primary point of the court's interest.

Judicial review of administrative decisions encompasses both the review of the redefined rules of procedure providing grounds for appraisal of the actual fact-finding mechanisms employed by an administration body required by law, and reviewing the manner of legal qualification of these facts, which applies to substantive and legal grounds for an administrative decision, including the review of legal interpretation performed by the body. In view of provisions of procedural acts stipulating legal requirements regarding reasoning of an administrative decision, this process involves reviewing the specific manner of determining factual and legal grounds for the decision in a given case.[94]

In the course of the proceedings, administrative court will re-examine the correctness of interpretation adopted by the administration body. In this sense, the court will itself interpret the law to determine competences of the administration body to adjudicate a case, procedural transactions to be taken during the process, and substantive aspects of the process and the final decision. During the judicial review, the administrative procedural law gets converted into substantive law, in the context of constructing the substance of a judicial decision. In place of a regular procedure of establishing the facts of a case on the other hand, the contested administrative decision is adopted, whereas what public administration body found as procedural grounds for making the decision, becomes the 'substantive law' for the court providing grounds for reviewing the manner in which the decision was taken.[95]

In the administrative process, an administration body is responsible for ensuring correctness of the validation and reconstruction findings. Therefore,

94 Compare L. Leszczyński, *Orzekanie przez sądy administracyjne a kontrola wykładni prawa*, "Zeszyty Naukowe Sądownictwa Administracyjnego", 5–6 (2010), , p. 267 and the following, and among others ruling of the VAC in Gdańsk of 2.10.2012, I SA/Gd 809/12, CBOSA; ruling of the SAC of 29.08.2012, II FSK 211/11, CBOSA.

95 More in: L. Leszczyński. *Stosowanie i wykładnia prawa administracyjnego*... op. cit., p. 10.

administrative court will investigate whether sources of law used by the administration body to interpret the legal rules comprising the grounds for initiating and conducting the law administration process and for issuing the decision closing the process, as well as reasoning adopted in the interpretation, were properly selected. At the same time, it should be noted that the administrative court is not bound by the limits of the lodged complaint and it should adopt its own reasoning to evaluate whether the decision and the process conducted to issue the decision meets the lawfulness requirement.

As regards the validation findings, the court will analyze the sources of law considered or bound to be considered while establishing legal grounds of the decision. Depending on specific facts of a given case, we can deal with simple circumstances when the body can match normative facts without too much difficulty or with circumstances with more or less complex validation findings. At the same time, it should be stressed that beside specific facts of a given case, the significance of specific sources laying normative grounds for the decision will be additionally determined by a branch of administrative law according to which the decision is made. In all branches, the prevailing role as a validation argument is by all means assigned to legal provisions. Depending on a given branch however, higher significance shall be given to provisions of the domestic (including local) law, or provisions of the international or Community law. What is more, specific branches may assign different significance to other administrative decisions and non-legal criteria; e.g. they shall be of lower significance in the light of the tax law or law on higher education. While determining the sources of law to be applied to a given decision-making process, administrative court will take into account systemic relationships between different sources, in particular between legal provisions.

As regards establishing the facts of a case, apart from checking whether sources of the legal grounds for the decision were properly selected, judicial review will also verify relevance of its substance. It will examine the redefinition process and its final outcome in the form of an applicable norm. Therefore, it will be necessary to determine whether an administration body used applicable rules of interpretation in a proper manner. While reviewing lawfulness of an administrative decision, the court will also examine whether legal grounds for the decision were correctly redefined. To that end, the court will interpret the normative facts to determine the applicable rule, and it will compare it with the rule that served as the basis for issuing the administrative decision. To do that, the court will use the whole spectrum of interpretation rules. Due to the fact that administration bodies define rights and obligations of individual entities by means of administrative acts, judicial review of proper interpretation of legal provisions, including extra-statutory provisions, is invaluable despite primarily cassation-like competences of these courts.[96]

It should be remembered that the purpose of administrative court proceedings is not an administrative case, but investigation of compliance of the contested act or transaction with the law. Therefore, administrative court is not an appellate authority, and administrative court proceedings do not continue administrative proceedings. Hence, the essence of public administration performance review is to settle an administrative case understood as an administrative dispute between an entity (addressee of the decision issued by public administration body) and the public administration body (author of the decision addressed to the entity) instigated before the court. The subject matter of this dispute is the plea in law against a public administration body. Resolution of this dispute by an administrative court comes down to a yes or no answer, that is confirmation of compliance or non-compliance of a given act with the law, which consequently means upholding it as valid or eliminating it from legal transactions. Consequently, the effect of the adjudication does not amount to specification of a legal norm, but to re-examining its interpretation and outcomes produced by an administration body, in consideration of the lawfulness criterion. As a result of the review process, administrative court is entitled to apply the measures prescribed by law.[97] The final outcome of the judicial review is the conclusion of "correctness" or "incorrectness" of administrative proceedings or substance of an administrative decision. Effects of adopting one of the above conclusions are stipulated in the valid legal norms. Applying these conclusions to provisions of the Code of Administrative Courts Procedure, it should be said that administrative courts are allowed to deliver a ruling dismissing the complaint (art. 151 of the Code of Administrative Courts Procedure), if it finds no infringements of the law or infringement to the extent justifying the interference, or it can uphold the complaint (art. 145–150 of the Code of Administrative Courts Procedure), if it finds the interference as absolutely substantiated and necessary. Upholding the complaint results in reversal of the administrative decision (in whole or in part), annulment (in whole or in part), or concluding that the decision was issued contrary to the law.

---

96 W. Jakimowicz, *Wykładnia w prawie administracyjnym*, Warszawa 2006, p. 481.

97 Compare T. Woś, H. Knysiak-Molczyk, M. Romańska, *Prawo o postępowaniu przed sądami administracyjnymi. Komentarz*, Warszawa 2005, p. 17.

2.3 Classification of case law impacts on making administrative decisions – judgement as 'restraint', 'driver' and 'guide-post'

The analysis of various systems and models of judicial review of administration makes it possible to classify impacts of rulings on reasoning of administration entities and on substance of their rulings. Classification of these impacts proposed below is universal and independent of any specific legal solutions based on legal transactions binding in specific countries, including of the adopted model of judicial review of administrative decisions (solely reversal and remanding competences of the court, or in conjunction with different forms of ruling reformulation). These legal regulations and models may however affect the scope (extensiveness and gravity) and the scale of case-law impact on public administration performance, which are different for different systems. This however, does not impact the conclusions below.

The first possible classification is the division into direct and indirect impact. The former refers to a possible direct influence of a ruling on a specific administrative decision. This includes all instances in which the court, with substance or reasoning of the ruling, can impact the process of making a single decision in a case that was the subject matter of a legal action. This refers to situations where as a result of a ruling, an administrative case is to be re-examined by an authority. Therefore, these include reversals (cassation) of administrative decisions by the court, instead of their replacement with decisions as to the merits. The latter may, on the other hand, indirectly impact issuing of decisions in other cases with corresponding facts of a case. As a rule, direct influence involves formal binding of an authority with findings or appraisals of facts and/or legal appraisals made by the court in the reasons for the ruling.

Indirect impact, on the other hand, takes place in all circumstances in which the court has no direct influence on the process of making a specific administrative decision. This involves situations where the authority refers to a ruling related to a different decision-making process than the one for which the contested decision was made. Most often, this will include decisions issued for similar facts of a case, in reference to an analogical legal basis used by the same authority. Then, having knowledge about previous judicial settlements in similar cases, the authority will refer (intentionally or unintentionally) to appraisals and arguments formulated in a ruling. Due to direct access to materials of a case, and consequently, to findings made by the court in relation to specific facts of a case, while examining a 'similar' case the authority will take into account previous rulings. This impact is independent of whether as a result of judicial review, the contested decision was upheld or reversed. In the first case, the authority specifically confirms correctness of the substance of the decision (ruling) it has formulated, and the relevant decision-making process becomes legitimized. In the other, the authority receives feedback from the court with indication of mistakes made during proceeding with the case subject to the review. Having knowledge (which will be discussed in greater detail in the final section hereof) about appraisals and findings made by the court, the authority will be able to quite safely determine to what extent the projected decision will comply with resolutions of the court in another case. This, in conjunction with findings of the authority regarding similarities and differences between the facts of both cases, will allow to respond to the question about potential risk of reversal (or amendment, should court adjudication be possible) of the newly projected decision.

Indirect impact is a non-formal impact including all cases in which the authority is not legally bound by any court findings, but irrespectively of that refers to these findings (whether or not this is revealed in the reasons for the administrative decision). Of course, the authority is under no formal obligation to take them into account, and it may make different findings – even in a highly similar case. As a rule however, at the stage of searching for the legal grounds for a future administrative decision, it should consider to what extent the earlier ruling is still valid in relation to the administrative case pending.

Notwithstanding the lack of direct formal binding with the court findings, usually due to the absence of a legal rule obliging the body to such conduct, in another administrative case one may also observe a para-formal binding. This namely involves the need to pursue fundamental democratic values, that is dependability (foreseeability) of the law and its application, and building civil trust to state agencies. Therefore, in the ruling of the Provincial Administrative Court in Cracow of 21st September 2009,[98] the court duly concludes that: "*The Polish legal system provides for no rule of precedence; however, since the authority adjudicated otherwise for nearly the same facts of a case, then it is obliged, the more so that this is raised in the appeal, to explain why it changes its position or for what reason the previous position cannot be applied to the considered case*".

In addition, it should be noted that any reference to rulings delivered in other cases can be prescribed by different circumstances. This, among others, results from different functions of judicial review of public administration

98 Ruling of the VAC in Kraków of 21.09.2009, II SA/Kr 1247/09, CBOSA.

performance. For the basic goal and outcome of this review, is to eliminate from the binding legal regime any non-complying acts and transactions pursued by public administration bodies, and to restore the legally binding transactions (irrespective of detailed solutions in this respect adopted in accordance with a given legal system). In this manner, a repressive function of the judicial review is revealed, significant both from the point of view of the appellant and the entire administration, which should be interested in eliminating any illegal acts and transactions of the officials from legal transactions. For lawfulness and regularity of transactions conducted by public administration bodies is a highly significant component of effective operation of the legal system and a prerequisite for social approval of the operation of the entire administration. The extent to which administration performance is approved directly impinges on the general and detailed appraisal of the overall functioning of the state. Apart from the repressive function, the preventive function of judicial review is equally important. It is intended to prevent future infringements of the law by public administration bodies. This goal may be pursued in two ways: firstly, various legal measures may be used to that end, intended to prevent similar breach of the law in the future. Secondly, similar impact is exerted by building social awareness of an independent authority reviewing performance of public administration that is equipped with repressive measures. Impact of both these functions leads to unification of the interpretation and application of administrative law provisions by public administration bodies.

Realization of direct and indirect impact of rulings on decision-making processes in state agencies reveals two perspectives: the micro and macro impact. The former involves a single administrative case and its outcome in the form of a final administrative decision. Realization of this impact allows to adopt an interesting point of view for the analysis, where one can observe how rulings affect specific reasoning of an administrative entity in relation to established facts and legal findings and their classification, as well as to the substance of an administrative decision, especially when the body is free to decide about the direction and/or scope of ruling (e.g. if the decision is based on administrative approval). The macro impact on the other hand, allows to analyze the relationships between the case-law (specifically determined and stable line of ruling) and establishment of the administration policy construed as a fixed manner of proceeding in specific cases, or protection of human rights and freedoms. This impact may be realized both in relation to decision-making processes within a single administration body, or different bodies operating in a task- or hierarchy-dependent system. The micro and macro impacts will serve as the starting point for analyses conducted in the following two sections hereof.

Case-law impact may be decision-driven or argument-driven. In the first case, it is about impact which is exerted by the judicial settlement on reasoning of the administration body or the substance of an administrative decision. Here, the reasons (arguments) of the ruling are of secondary importance. The key issue for the administration body is the conclusion which impacts the decision-making process with varied power. Differences in the power depend on many factors, surely including legal binding with appraisals included in such a ruling (direct impact situations), and cases in which the body will refer to the ruling, e.g. for pragmatic reasons, in order to avoid the risk of potential reversal or amendment (depending on adopted model of judicial review of administrative performance) of the decision made (indirect impact situations). In the latter, it is about instances when the body (its office holder) fearing, e.g. a negative opinion about its performance by an entity that selected or appointed it, will make informed decisions that stand a chance of being upheld as a result of any possible appeal. For the administration body, arguments and reasons for the ruling will be of secondary importance here, as the primary significance will be assigned to the settlement. This of course shall not preclude the body to use the argument-based level/tier of the ruling. In practice, this means that both decision- and argument-driven impact of the court on public administration performance may be similar (of similar power), or higher importance may be assigned to either of them. In the case of argument-driven impact on the administrative decision maker and its reasoning, the primary significance is assigned to motifs presented in the reasons for the ruling. The arguments may speak in favour of reasonableness of the ruling (indicating its correctness) or refer to a larger extent to the process of issuing an administrative decision. As a rule, these will be arguments formulated for a given case, however more general arguments may often appear as well. In this manner, argument-driven impact may refer to a given administrative case or more broadly to other cases examined by a given body, or even by the entire administration.

An analysis of administrative decision-making processes and models of judicial review of administration performance, as well as case-law impact on the reasoning of administration entities and the line of delivered rulings, allows to establish a figurative classification of impacts taking the form of a "brake", "motivator" and "signpost". At the same time, they all permeate and complement each other. They differ in terms of their scope and scale (which is discussed in greater detail in the following sections) in the particular phases of the decision-making process in public administration, or in terms of their impact on establishment of administration policies.

The "brake" involves all cases where the court reviewing administration performance provides for a kind of a "wall" protecting the entity – the less powerful entity in a typical administrative relationship – and its rights against issuing of an arbitrary decision infringing on human rights and freedoms, and protecting the legal order against issuing of an unlawful decision. Acting as a "brake" may involve instances of direct and indirect impact on the process of issuing an administrative decision. It may also be analyzed from the micro and macro points of view. It involves both situations where the court shall remove from the legal order a decision non-complying with verification criteria adopted in accordance with a specific system, as well as generally instances of decisions made in circumstances in which, e.g. due to the principle of proportionality, it was possible to adopt another (less authoritative and invasive) form of handling a given case than an administrative decision, or implementation of an administrative task.

Ruling as the "motivator" is the reverse of the latter aspect. It refers to instances in which the body was obliged, in the legal or factual sense, to take specific actions, including e.g. to issue an administrative decision but it failed to do so or extended this in time. Then a ruling is supposed to motivate the body, most often by adoption of an authoritative ruling. This may take the form of a direct or indirect influence. It may be analyzed in relation to the motivating function – by the argument-based level of the ruling, the court motivates the body to work out specific reasoning (its scope and significance) concerning establishment of the facts of a case, interpretation of legal grounds for the decision, or justification of the decision taken.

The latter coincides with the function of case-law as the "signpost" for public administration. The court becomes this signpost in all situations in which it either directly indicates the manner in which to perceive and construe specific, case-relevant, factual and legal phenomena, or it indirectly indicates the manner in which this should be done or in which a given body should do it.

Either of the a/m three forms of case-law impact on public administration performance can be traced in any case and in reference to any stage of law application, however some of them shall play a more significant role in specific situations than other, and this will be shown in the next section hereof. For it is about showing the actual impact of the court on an administration body and on the reasoning it adopts while applying the law, which lead to formulation of the final decision with specific substance.

In this manner, we arrive at the last of the proposed divisions, that is actual and legal impact. The latter employs all instances where an administrative body is legally bound to refer to or (more strongly) take into account the findings, appraisals and arguments stated in the ruling. With certain simplification, it can be stated that these include all instances of formal impact described above. Actual impact will take place in any case in which the body will refer to and, even to the minimum extent, make use of a decision or argument provided in the case-law in relation to the entire process, its specific stages or more broadly, to the decision-making policy. In this sense, the actual impact also includes all instances of legal effect. It is not applicable however, to situations in which the body refers to a ruling but fails to make use of it to any extent. In such a case, we cannot speak about any impact on public administration, notwithstanding difficulties with distinguishing such situations.

Part III. Microscale of influence – impact on a single decision

3.1 Influence on process commencement

As mentioned in chapter I, the commencement of the law application process occurs at the moment of the occurrence of a decision-making situation that is the moment of co-existence of a legal standard potentially underlying the action of the administering body and a relevant (in the opinion of the legislature or the body itself) fact that implies lines of reasoning aimed at answering the question about effects caused or that should be caused by the statement of its occurrence. Therefore, a decision-making situation arises at the moment of the occurrence of a fact (irrespectively of its type and source) that, in the light of competencies granted to the body or tasks entrusted to it, causes or should cause specific legal effects. One of such effects can include undertaking of an action to issue an individual administrative act. Undertaking such action can be determined by an obligation imposed by the legislature or it can depend on the will of the body. If the legislature formulated such an obligation or if necessary, in the opinion of the body, the occurrence of a decision-making situation leads to the making of a decision to start the law application process that also becomes the first fragmentary decision of that process. Therefore, the administrative type of the law application process commences at the moment of the issue of a decision to initiate it as an effect of the occurrence of a decision-making situation.

Such reasoning occurs as a part of the pre-decision phase that determines the existence of the entire law application process. Additionally, if a body makes a decision to commence the process, the decision-making situation (findings made as its part), will become the first phase of that process and the decision to commence it will be the first fragmentary decision. All the findings made during that phase of the process will then become of interest to the body.

The decision to commence the law application process can be determined by the legislature that can mention unambiguous consequences of the occurrence of specific facts in the social reality in the contents of legal standards in force. In that case, the obligation to act in connection with the appearance of such a fact is imposed on the body. Situations in which the legislature leaves freedom in that area to the administration body are also possible. Therefore, it is possible to distinguish two groups of decision-making situations: when the occurrence of a specific fact implies the obligation to examine the case in the light of legal standards in force (first group) and when the decision concerning the potential commencement of the process depends on the body itself (second group).

The first group covers all cases in which the body will have no freedom of decision regarding the making of a decision to commence the law application process. It is because the occurrence of a fact that is relevant from the perspective of a legal standard (automatically) implies the need to take further actions regarding the case. Lack of the body's reaction or undertaking an action other than the one specified in the legal standard equals its violation.

In turn, the second group is particularly important from the perspective of the subject of this publication in the light of the freedom of decision related to it. In such situations, the administering entity is authorized in the light of legal standards in force to issue a binding unit legal decision but is not obliged to do it as in the first group of situations. It is because a settlement order does not apply and the freedom of decision is related to the possibility of choice between commencing and not commencing the process. Therefore, these are the cases when it depends on the evaluation made by the decision-making entity, i.e. on its subjective belief, whether the law application process will commence or not.

The administering entity will be free to make a decision to commence the decision-making process in those situations when the legislature entrusts specific tasks to it but does not indicate the method of their execution. In such a situation, the body is obliged to choose the action that attains the determined goal as fully as possible considering the complex conditions in which it operates and means it has at its disposal. The public administration has to take action in the name of the fulfilment of tasks imposed on it and, to this end, should take advantage of legal forms of action vested in it.[99] In such a decision-making situation, the entity has a legally permitted range of potential actions and specific knowledge of the reality surrounding it. Appropriate knowledge and experience will make it possible to that entity to specify (rather generally) effects that each of the potential actions can cause. On that basis, the body should select an action that will be optimal (in its opinion) from the perspective of the intended task and available resources. Such actions can include the issue of a decision to apply the law (one or more decisions) subject to the fact that it is a legally admissible action, i.e. there is a competence standard in the law system that authorizes the body to behave in this manner. It is the so-called subjectively perceived necessity to commence the process.

---

99 More in: J. Filipek, *Rola prawa w działalności administracyjnej państwa*, „Zeszyty Naukowe Uniwersytetu Jagiellońskiego – Prace Prawnicze“ 1974, book 65, p. 53.

The subjectively perceived necessity to commence the law application process occurs when the need to complete a task is an impulse for action for the administering entity. Such a necessity can be caused due to a range of external (e.g. a change of the administration policy, body operations control carried out by a body that is superior in the hierarchy or a political option that selected the office holder), internal (e.g. reorganization of the administering entity improving the effectiveness of its external operations and enabling the undertaking of tasks it could not have executed before, e.g. due to limited staff resources) or personal factors (e.g. personal ambitions and aspirations of the office holder).

The subjectivity of conditions determining the situation manifests with the lack of its full determination with the legislature's intent, which is the case in the first and second group of decision-making situations. However, it does not mean that the decision-maker can take any action. The legislature specifies certain limits of its lines of reasoning by defining the goal for the attainment of which the administration body should strive and by specifying legal forms in which its goals can be realized, including the granting of competence to issue individual law application acts in specific types of cases and indicating values (axiology) it should take into account. At the same time, it is up to the body to evaluate how it will want to execute a task and whether it will take advantage of the related right to issue a law application decision.

An administering entity willing to choose an optimum action has to evaluate legally permitted possibilities of task execution on the basis of specified criteria. If the legislature does not impose such criteria the scope of freedom shall be wider and include the possibility to choose the leading evaluation criterion. The body shall pursue all these lines of reasoning in complex socioeconomic realities, in a rapidly changing reality. It will lead to a situation in which the contents of a specific settlement, including a decision to commence the law application process, shall be influenced (or, at least, could be influenced) by a range of non-legal factors. Freedom in this area is limited first by legal standards in force: on the one hand, competence standards whose presence in the system is necessary in order to be able to consider the possibility of starting the process leading to the issue of a sovereign unilateral settlement in an external sphere and, on the other hand, law principles and axiology of the legal system.

Therefore, a question appears about the importance of rulings of the courts controlling the administration at the moment of the occurrence of a decision-making situation relating to the first and second group. In judicial control systems based on the legality criterion, the potential influence of prior court rulings is minor at the analyzed moment of the decision-making process. When we look at the first group of situations, judicial control is limited to the zero-one statement whether a public administration body took action in line with the contents of a legal standard that ordered its undertaking at the moment of an occurrence of a specific fact (e.g. submission of a motion to the body that, in the light of regulations of the Polish Code of Administrative Procedures, entails the obligation to formally commence an administrative procedure but does not determine its completion). In other words: has the public administration body reacted properly to the fact assuming that its reaction type is clearly predefined in the form of an imperative standard.

In turn, if we analyze the second group of decision-making situations we will have to conclude that the greater margin of freedom available to the administering entity when making decisions to commence the law application process, including the point of gravity for the verification of the way in which such freedom is used, the further moves the balance point of verification of the manner in which that freedom is used – from the strictly juridical argumentation to the non-legal one. Obviously, it does not mean that the legality principle loses its priority in the evaluation of such decisions. In those cases when the body can choose the means to settle a case, it should determine whether an administrative decision is the most appropriate form or whether there is a way that will not limit the rights and freedoms of an individual according to the proportionality principle. The influence of the latter entails the need to take three points of evaluation of the planned action into account, namely: usefulness (the ability of the measure to attain the defined goal), necessity (the interference cannot go beyond what is necessary to attain a goal), maintenance of a good relationship between the goal of an action and the burden and severity of applied measures.[100]

100 More in: Z. Kmieciak, *Ogólne zasady prawa i postępowania administracyjnego*, Warszawa 2000, pp. 111–116. For more about the proportionality principle, see the CT ruling of 28.06.2000, K 34/99, LEX No. 41213.; D. Kijowski, *Zasada adekwatności w prawie administracyjnym*, „Państwo i Prawo" 1990, book 4, pp. 59–68; J. Zakolska, *Zasada proporcjonalności w orzecznictwie Trybunału Konstytucyjnego*, Warszawa 2008, passim; P. Pietrasz, *Zasada proporcjonalności a postępowanie administracyjne*, [in:] *Kodyfikacja postępowania administracyjnego na 50-lecie K.P.A.*, ed. J. Niczyporuk, Lublin 2010, pp. 637–642. A similar position was also taken in the already referenced recommendation No. R (80) 2 of the Committee of Ministers of the Council of Europe of 11 March 1980 that recommends retaining an appropriate balance between the result of a decision in the area of rights, freedoms and interests of individuals and the intended goal of the procedure. The proportionality principle also found its expression in the European Code of Good Administration. See: J. Świątkiewicz, *Europejski Kodeks Dobrej Administracji – wprowadzenie, tekst i komentarz o zastosowaniu kodeksu w warunkach polskich procedur administracyjnych*, Warszawa 2007, pp. 23–24.

Legality and proportionality are principles that most strongly of all principles determine the scope of freedom available to the entity applying the law at the stage of the decision to commence the process. On the one hand, legal standards define cases in which a body is obliged to take specific action or give a body specific discretionary power in that area. On the other hand, in those situations when it has at least minimal freedom, it should carry out a proportionality test to learn whether the intended decision-making process would lead to the attainment of the assumed goal, whether it is necessary in the light of the public interest and whether its effect in the form of a decision would be commensurate with the resulting limitations.

The Polish administrative court rulings worked out a clear position according to which, if a goal is attainable with the use of another measure imposing lesser limitations on rights and freedoms the use of a stricter measure exceeds what is necessary and, therefore, violates the Constitution.[101] From that perspective, the commencement of the law application process aimed at the issue of a decision for a unit addressee is subject to verification by independent courts. Courts, in turn, do not verity the passivity of the public administration when it comes to the execution of tasks. The latter can be evaluated by specific political powers, organizational structures of the administration and the society.

Therefore, considering the totality of possible decision-making situations and the range of decision-making freedom available to administering bodies at this stage of the process, one has to conclude that court rulings constitute a "brake" for a public administration body on the one hand and, on the other hand, a "motivator" at the stage of the issue of a decision to start the process aimed at the issue of an administrative decision. In situations belonging to the second group and related to a subjective evaluation of grounds for the commencement of the law application process, it is a barrier for the selection of an action that would violate the axiology of the legal order, in particular, the proportionality principle referring to the protection of individual rights in a democratic state under the rule of law. Therefore, thanks to established jurisprudence, it can prevent situations in which a body interested in the contents of an action shall "sacrifice" the legally protected good of an individual in the light of the necessity to execute tasks it has to account for. Obviously, the related judicial control is of secondary nature, i.e. it takes place after the issue of a decision and after the completion

101 Among other things, see the CT ruling of 12.01.2000, sign. P 11/98, LEX No. 39282; CT ruling of 10.04.2002, K 26/00, LEX No. 54052; CT ruling of 13.09.2007, K 8/07, LEX No. 257767; CT rulings of 24.11.2008, K 66/07, LEX No. 464925.

of appeal proceedings. However, when coupled with the subsequent possibility to lodge claims against the body under the civil law, it can be a material argument to be considered at the stage of the issue of a decision to examine a case. However, if we look at the first group of decision-making situations, i.e. when the body is legally obliged to take specific action as a reaction to the occurrence of a fact specified in the legal standard, the rulings of administrative courts will be an impulse preventing the passivity of a body. The possibility to complain to the court against an idleness of a body[102] prevents cases in which a body should take specific steps but fails to do so and an entity has no other possibility to claim its rights.

The influence of rulings of administrative courts is direct in the pre-decision phase, especially in proceedings initiated by a specific body after the issue of a ruling stating the idleness of the body or a violation of the proportionality principle. At the same time, it is a decision-making influence, i.e. it relates to the essence of the court ruling rather than the argumentation formulated in its statement of reasons.

Finally, it should be mentioned that certain decisions of administering entities made at the pre-decision stage can escape not only the judicial verification but also the instance verification provided by other public administration bodies. The institution of a "tacit agreement of a body" can be an example found in the current legal status prevailing in Poland.[103] It applies in those cases where the idleness of a body equals the approval from the legal perspective. The institution of the notification of intention to commence construction works adopted by the Polish legislature in the building law can be an example of that type of the decision-making process.[104] After such notification is submitted, the body

---

102 In Poland, such a possibility is provided for in the act of 30 August 2002 – the Law of Administrative Courts Procedure (Dz.U.2017.1369 c.t).

103 See: A. Kubiak, *Fikcja pozytywnego rozstrzygnięcia w prawie administracyjnym*, „Państwo i Prawo" 2009, no. 11, pp. 32–46 (the author uses the term "fiction of positive resolution"); polemics in T. Bąkowski, *W sprawie „milczącej zgody organu"*, „Państwo i Prawo" 2010, no. 3, pp. 107–110 and A. Kubiak, *O fikcji pozytywnego rozstrzygnięcia administracji raz jeszcze*, „Państwo i Prawo" 2010, no. 5, pp. 100–106. The term "tacit consent of the body" is also used in the ruling practice, e.g. see the ruling of the VAC in Olsztyn of 25.06.2013, II SA/Ol 251/13, CBOSA; ruling of the VAC in Warsaw of 11.06.2013, VIII SA/Wa 144/13, CBOSA; ruling of the VAC in Lublin of 14.03.2013, II SA/Lu 8/13, CBOSA. Ruling of the VAC in Lublin of 26.02.2013, II SA/Lu 61/13, CBOSA: "[…] due to the non-juridical nature of the tacit consent of the body accepting the planned investment in this manner it is not possible to undermine it in the appeal or in extraordinary modes […]".

104 The act of 7 July 1994 r. – Building Law (Dz.U. of 2013 No. 1409 ct).

checks the action for compliance with applicable standards of the substantive law and can submit an objection in the form of an administrative decision within 30 days. The failure to submit an objection within that term entails the consent to the execution of intended investments specified in the notification. In such cases, there is no formal commencement of the administrative procedure regulated in the Code of Administrative Procedures but the law application process is commenced and completed. A body took action reacting to the notification submitted by a party and, in the light of the lack of grounds for an objection in the situation, it decided (informally) not to submit such an objection.

Such a model of the decision-making process results from the concept currently adopted under the administrative law that grants an individual the legal capacity to take substantive actions modelling its rights or obligations. The sovereignty of a public administration body is limited in such cases to the control of the legality of the entity's activities. Such legal solutions can lead to the working out of an administrative procedure concept in a wide sense not traditionally related to the multitude of forms of activity of the public administration but rather to substantive activities of the entity and their control by administration bodies.[105]

The discussed example shows that the submission of an application will result in the commencement of the law application process and the body will be obliged to take action aimed at the verification of facts indicated there. It will not always equal the commencement of the administrative procedure. If a submission made pursuant to provisions of the building law is considered compliant with legal standards the body shall complete the law application process without the commencement of the administrative procedure.[106] In that case, the decision to refuse to initiate the administrative procedure due to the lack of grounds for it will be a decision ending the law application process. A potential non-compliance with the law of an action taken by a party will result in the commencement of the administrative procedure *ex officio* as a reaction to the facts. Additionally, an entity cannot submit an application concerning the idleness of the body in such situations. In turn, filing an objection in the form of an administrative decision

105 B. Adamiak, *Zagadnienia ogólne procesowego prawa administracyjnego*, [in:] *System prawa administracyjnego, vol. 9: Prawo procesowe administracyjne*, eds. R. Hauser, Z. Niewiadomski, A. Wróbel, Warszawa 2010, p. 4.

106 Among others, the ruling of the VAC in Lublin of 26.02.2013, II SA/Lu 61/13, CBOSA also indicates the non-juridical nature of the "tacit consent of the body".

can be subject to further administrative court verification but it will apply to stages of the law application process other than the pre-decision phase.

3.2 Determination of facts of an administrative case

During the determination of facts, the body will have to do with two groups of facts: drivers for the commencement of the decision-making process (determined in the pre-decision phase) and facts with an impact on its progress and completion (determined in the decision-making phase). The range of necessary findings in both fact groups is determined under legal standards in force that also specify consequences of their statement. Facts determined at the pre-decision stage will become facts of the case as soon as the decision to commence the law application process is made. Throughout the process, the decision-making entity will determine facts specified in standards in force or facts on the basis of which, in the light of such standards, the entity can or should draw specific conclusions. The entire process will take place according to a formalized procedure. As S. Wronkowska and Z. Ziembiński observe, the determination of facts is a conventional action of major legal importance, undertaken according to specified rules on the basis of evidence taken as provided under the law.[107] It means that the determination of facts of the case takes place in conjunction with the validation and interpretation reasoning, which allows the entity to specify the range of facts to be proven in the case. The rules of the substantive law in force specify the catalogue of facts of the case that have to be determined prior to the issue of a decision regarding a specific case.

In the initial phase of the decision-making process, the body has to identify the likelihood of an occurrence of the fact that implies the need (in an objectivized or subjectively perceived sense) to commence the process and, after that, to conduct the administrative procedure and issue a decision. The administrative procedure regulated under the Code of Administrative Procedures will be aimed at their verification in order to issue a substantive decision.

Legal standards specify a passive or an active attitude of the body in the light of the information about facts of the case and, in particular, whether and to what extent the body is bound with the supplied information and to what extent it can strive to obtain it.[108] The determination of facts in law application processes can

107 S. Wronkowska, Z. Ziembiński, *Zarys teorii prawa*, Poznań 1997, p. 219.

108 More in: W. Lang, J. Wróblewski, S. Zawadzki, *Teoria państwa i prawa*, Warszawa 1979, p. 424.

be based on the material truth principle or the formal truth principle (or their combination). However, irrespectively of the related detailed preferences of the legislature, it has to be concluded that the determination of actual facts is the obligation resulting from the ideology of the lawful application of the law and the belief in the procedural completeness of the law system.[109]

Provisions of the Code of Administrative Procedures in force in Poland leave no doubts in that area by stating that administration bodies, in the course of the procedure, aim at the accurate clarification of the facts (art. 7 of the Code of Administrative Procedures) by way of the exhaustive collection and examination of the entire evidence (art. 77 of the Code of Administrative Procedures). The objective truth principle is one of the leading principles of the administrative procedure while other general principles are designed to create such conditions in the course of the procedure that will make it possible to determine true facts. The correct determination of facts prejudges the rationality of the issued decision.[110] The adoption of the material truth principle as governing the process of the determination of facts determines the body's activities in that area to a great degree, i.e. the body has to strive to determine all facts material for the case in a complete manner. It is even more so as the evidence taking procedure serves the clarification of the case in line with the obligation to reach the objective truth but all the circumstances that enable the expression of the reason of public interest and legitimate interest of the parties have to be determined as well when settling the case.[111]

Due to its direct interest in the issued decision, the body can strive to determine only those facts that will justify the issue of a decision having specific contents. In this respect, the objective truth principle protects a party from a non-objective and illegal activity of an administration body. It also rules out the body's arbitrariness in that area. At the same time, all the actions taken by the body need to have a legal basis and consider the circumstances invoked by a party.[112]

Determination of facts in law application processes has to be analyzed from two interrelated perspectives: the first perspective refers to the determination of

---

109 See: B. Wojciechowski, *Dyskrecjonalność sędziowska…*, op. cit., p. 124 and more in the literature referenced there.

110 Similarly, among others, the SC ruling of 23.11.1994, III ARN 55/94, LEX No. 9409.

111 More: J. Borkowski, *Postępowanie zwykłe. Przedmiot postępowania zwykłego*, [in:] *System prawa administracyjnego, vol. 9: Prawo procesowe administracyjne*, eds. R. Hauser, Z. Niewiadomski, A. Wróbel, Warszawa 2010, p. 147.

112 Among other things, the ruling of the SAC in Wrocław of 6.11.1994, SA/Wr 806/93, CBOSA.

facts of the case and the other one refers to their correct evaluation. Therefore, the process can be referred to two types of reasoning: determination of the existence or non-existence of certain facts in the social reality and the evaluation of their importance for the case.

The administrative procedure aims at the determination of facts of the case that, in the light of legal standards in force, will make it possible to issue a unit decision. In addition to the facts that should be determined before the end of the process, the legislature also indicates which body should collect them. Two issues are of key importance, i.e. the scope of determination of facts of the case and the procedure according to which it should take place. In other words, questions that should be answered are: what evidence the body has to reach for during the determination of facts of the case and according to which procedure this process should take place?

According to art. 75 § 1 of the Code of Administrative Procedures, "everything that can contribute to the clarification of the case and is not illegal has to be admitted as evidence".[113] Additionally, the legislature lists the following examples of evidence pursuant to the said regulation: documents, witnesses' testimonies, experts' opinions and visual inspection. It is an open catalogue of evidence permitted in the administrative procedure and there is no hierarchy in it. It means that facts of the case can also be demonstrated with the use of evidence other than the evidence mentioned in the regulation. In its ruling of 1984, the SAC stated: "The realization of the objective truth requires that everything that can contribute to the clarification of facts and is not contrary to the law should be permitted as evidence in the case".

The entity applying the law decides upon the selection of specific evidence and it can choose the evidence mentioned in the Code of Administrative Procedures or use evidence not included in that catalogue. However, such freedom is limited, e.g. when the legislature indicates specific evidence that the body should take in order to determine the existence of specific facts.

---

113 The concept of "evidence" is ambiguous. More: M. Podleśny, *Zasada prawdy obiektywnej w postępowaniu administracyjnym*, [in:] *Kodyfikacja postępowania administracyjnego na 50-lecie K.P.A.*, ed. J. Niczyporuk, Lublin 2010, pp. 645–655. For the needs of this work, it was adopted after B. Adamiak that the concept equals the concept of the "evidentiary measure" understood as all sources of the true information enabling the argumentation. More: B. Adamiak, *System środków w ogólnym postępowaniu administracyjnym*, „Annales Universitatis Wratislaviensis – Przegląd Prawa i Administracji" 1984, R. XVIII, p. 47.

The assessment of facts can be analyzed from two perspectives: 1) as the evaluation of the reliability and sufficiency of evidence in order to demonstrate a specific circumstance and 2) as assessments formulated by the body in connection with the existence of assessment statements in the legal system. Related freedom of the body has to be referred, on the one hand, to the freedom of assessment of evidence (1) and, on the other hand, to the determination of the occurrence of facts expressed as an assessment by the legislature (2).[114]

Free assessment of evidence does not equal discretion. The assessment of evidence taken should be based on convincing grounds and reflected in an appropriate statement of reasons.[115] The judicature[116] and the doctrine[117] indicate a range of requirements that the process of assessment of facts of the case should meet. In its ruling of 17.05.1994, the SAC[118] indicated explicitly that in order not to become arbitrary, the free assessment of evidence has to take place in line with standards of the procedural law and subject to the rules of that assessment, i.e.:

---

114 In the ruling of 12.01.2010, the VAC in Warsaw (VII SA/Wa 1400/09, CBOSA) indicated that "bodies in the administrative proceedings are obliged to assess each piece of evidence taken. The bodies can consider each piece of evidence reliable or deny its reliability in full or in part. They have the right and the obligation to check whether the submitted opinion is complete, reliable and logical and, potentially, require its supplementation". The rule of the free assessment of evidence is introduced implicitly in art. 80 of the Code of Administrative Procedures. It refers both to the assessment of individual facts, the entire material of the case and to individual facts in the context of the entirety of the collected evidence.

115 E. Iserzon, J. Starościak, *Kodeks postępowania administracyjnego. Komentarz, teksty, wzory i formularze*, Warszawa 1970, p. 155.

116 Among other things, see the ruling of the VAC in Kraków of 19.09.2013, I SA/Kr 526/13, CBOSA; ruling of the VAC in Łódź of 17.09.2013, II SA/Łd 672/13, CBOSA; ruling of the VAC in Olsztyn of 25.09.2009, II SA/Ol 529/09, CBOSA; ruling of the VAC in Warsaw of 14.10.2004, III SA 949/03, CBOSA.

117 In this area, A. Hanusz formulated an interesting assumption related to tax procedures, indicating that "[...] when building the basis for the factual presumption, a tax body, according to the principle of the free assessment of evidence, can believe those or other indirect evidentiary facts and assess their value and evidentiary power directed by life experience, knowledge of management rules, natural laws and similar non-legal criteria". For more, see A. Hanusz, *Źródło domniemania faktycznego a orzecznictwo sądów administracyjnych w sprawach podatkowych*, „Zeszyty Naukowe Sądownictwa Administracyjnego" 2010, no. 5–6, pp. 143–155.

118 See the ruling of the SAC in Lublin of 17.051994, SA/Lu 1921/93, LEX No. 26517.

- firstly, it should be based on the evidence collected by the body subject to exemptions provided for in the laws;
- secondly, the assessment should be based on the end-to-end evaluation of the entire evidence;
- thirdly, the body should assess the importance and value of evidence for the pending case subject to limitations related to official documents that, pursuant to art. 76 § 1 of the Code of Administrative Procedures, have particular evidential power. A body can refuse to believe specific evidence only after its comprehensive examination and subject to the explanation of the reason for such an assessment;
- fourthly, the reasoning resulting in the body determining the existence of facts should comply with the rules of logic.

However, the assessment of facts of the case should be distinguished from the determination of the existence of facts that the legislature expressed in an assessing manner.[119] According to J. Wróblewski, the existence of facts distinguished descriptively in the law can be proven just like all existential statements in a non-legal area or it can be law-specific depending on the adopted evidence theories. He indicates that demonstrating such a fact does not require any assessments by assumption. The statement of the occurrence of facts expressed in an assessing manner requires more complex measure in order to determine their existence; it shall entail the statement of occurrence of a specific fact and its subsequent assessment.[120] The first of these components will be subjected to dependencies indicated above. The second one will provide an opportunity for the decision-making entity to consider non-legal criteria of the assessment of the ascertained fact. Such assessments will be made in the context of a specific case.[121]

---

119 Examples of the valuable approach to facts can include: "extraordinary circumstances", "justified cause", "blatant violation of the law", "particularly justified case".

120 More: J. Wróblewski, *Sądowe stosowanie prawa…* op. cit., pp. 190–192. More about assessing statements in the interpretation and application of the administrative law: L. Leszczyński, *Interpretacyjna rola kryteriów otwartych i innych decyzji stosowania prawa*, [in:] *System prawa administracyjnego*, vol. 4: *Wykładnia w prawie administracyjnym*, op. cit., pp. 340–345. Compare also the SAC ruling of 10.07.2012, II OSK 694/11, CBOSA; SAC ruling of 14.06.2011, II OSK 1092/10, CBOSA.

121 More: SC ruling of 17.03.2005, III PK 83/04, LEX 166420: "The assessment conducted by the court is a unit and situational assessment as it is conducted in a specific case and on the basis of a comparison of facts actually occurring in that case and "imagined"

The doctrine and jurisprudence stress that an assessment statement, being a normative statement, has an objective and knowable content and does not entail the expression of interpreter's own preferences or concealment of social or political evaluations.[122] However, it has to be noted that, in the case of decision-making processes led by administration bodies, the impact of such factors on an assessment cannot be ruled out. A body will always carry out such reasoning in a specific complex social and political situation that can more or less influence the result of its work. It will be a benchmark for the assessment of a fact and it can also indirectly and non-formally influence the assessment formulated by the body.

When looking at the collection and assessment of evidence in the administrative procedure from the perspective of control exercised by administrative courts, it has to be noted that the verification of the administration body's reasoning leading to the cognition of facts of the case refers to the checking how the body ascertained these facts, whether the collected material is complete and was correctly assessed. Finally, the way in which facts are "highlighted" in the statement of reasons for a decision is subjected to an evaluation. Therefore, it is checked whether the administering entity determined the facts with the use of legally permissible measures, in line with the procedure in force (including compliance with the rules and form of procedure), including the taking of entire evidence required under the law and determination of all facts of the case in line with the objective truth principle, in particular, the facts that it was obliged to determine under the legal standards in force and, finally, whether its assessment of individual facts and the entire material collected was correct and whether it stated the reasons for its decision in line with code requirements.

In the light of the fact that the verification of compliance of the administration's activities with legal standards is controlled by the administrative court, the court does not determine facts of the case again but rather analyses the way in which the body completed that task. Therefore, this "activity" is limited to the verification of correctness of findings made by the entity that issued a decision with no new evidence taking. Compliance with legal standards in force will be the basic evaluation criterion. The following components are subject to

---

facts that could occur in such cases". See also the SAC ruling of 20.01.2009, II OZ 1368/08, CBOSA.

122 More: L. Leszczyński, *Interpretacyjna rola kryteriów otwartych i innych decyzji stosowania prawa*, op. cit., p. 342. See the SAC ruling of 20.05.2010, II OPS 6/09, CBOSA See also: J. Harczuk, *Zwroty szacunkowe jako przesłanka przyznania prawa pomocy*, „Zeszyty Naukowe Sądownictwa Administracyjnego" 2007, no. 5–6.

the verification: checking whether the body violated the duty to take specific evidence or demonstrate a specific fact justifying the issue of a decision with specific contents if that body was obliged to take or demonstrate it under the standards in force. If there is no such duty (or if the duty was fulfilled) it is also ascertained whether the body determined facts of the case in line with the objective truth principle, i.e. whether it determined all facts potentially influencing the contents of the issued decision. Such verification also includes the checking of the procedure followed and findings related to the correct assessment of facts and their qualification in the context of the reconstructed normative basis of the decision. The legality control of above-mentioned findings is the field of main interest to the administrative court. It covers the verification of compliance of actions with legal standards and rules of administrative procedure. In its ruling of 19 November 2010, the SAC[123] indicated that the correctness of the determination of facts is within the scope of the legality assessment in the law application process and is subject to the review of the administrative court.

On the one hand, judicial review will cover the fulfilment of the body's duty to use specific evidence if the legislature provides for such an obligation and, on the other hand, the fulfilment of the requirement of determination of the actual status of the case and its correct assessment. It will be of key importance for the administrative court to check whether the body applying the law found the material truth on the basis of legally permissible measures[124] and created conditions for a party to take an active part in the procedure and whether it assessed facts of the case correctly. The latter becomes particularly important in the case of assessment statements occurring during the determination of facts.[125] In turn,

123 See the SAC ruling of 19.11.2010, I GSK 16/08, CBOSA.

124 In their ruling practice, courts challenge the reasonableness of admitting the evidence such as, e.g.: a post office chronicle, which is not an official document with a certain date (ruling of the SAC in Warsaw of 12.02.2002, I SA 1112/00, LEX No. 82665); official note (ruling of the SAC in Gdańsk of 21.11.2001, I SA/Gd 306/99, LEX No. 76108); a print of the expropriation decision without a date and the certification of its compliance with the original (ruling of the SAC in Warsaw of 19.11.2001, I SA 953/00, LEX No. 81996); not officially certified photocopies of documents (ruling of the SAC in Warsaw of 21.09.1999, III SA 7375/98, LEX No. 40052).

125 It is stressed in the ruling practice that the use of assessment statements in the determination of facts requires a detailed and convincing justification of the resolution indicating the selection of evaluation criteria. Compare the ruling of the SAC of 6.03.2012, I OSK 555/11, CBOSA; similarly the SAC ruling of 29.02.2012, II OSK 45/12, CBOSA, ruling of the SAC in Lublin of 7.10.2003, II SA/Lu 1115/03, CBOSA.

as regards the freedom to initiate the administrative procedure, the compliance with proportionality requirements will be additionally subject to verification.[126]

In particular, the court verifies whether all steps necessary to accurately clarify the facts were taken during the procedure. To this end, the method of collection and evaluation of all facts material for the case is verified. The evidence for the case should be collected in a complete and exhaustive manner and duly analyzed after that. The administration body should consider all circumstances that can influence the choice of the best settlement. It is also obliged to refer to all motions and allegations raised by a party. After that, results of the investigation procedure should be assessed within the limits of the free assessment of evidence on the basis of knowledge and principles of the experience of life.[127] The court should also check accurately whether the body determined all facts in the course of the procedure to determine the existence or non-existence of statutory premises of the issue of a discretionary decision or whether, pursuant to specific legal regulations, it was permitted in a specific case to issue a decision with a specific content.[128]

The assessment of correctness of the determination of fact has yet another dimension: results of the verification of correctness of findings made by the body applying the law will influence the evaluation of the use of other manifestations of discretionary power of the entity including, among other things, the administrative discretion.[129] While the court is unable to interfere with the scope of the

126 Among other things, see the decision of the VAC in Gdańsk of 7.11.2007, III SA/Gd 325/07, LEX No. 513827; ruling of the VAC in Warsaw of 17.03.2011, V SA/Wa 2821/10, LEX No. 996043; SAC ruling of 18.03.2011, II FSK 1801/09, LEX No. 821091. As A. Stępkowski observes (*Zasada proporcjonalności w europejskiej kulturze prawnej: sądowa kontrola władzy dyskrecjonalnej w nowoczesnej Europie*, Warszawa 2010, p. 324), administrative courts most frequently refer to the proportionality principle in tax cases.

127 See the ruling of the VAC in Rzeszów of 6.04.2009, I SA/Rz 788/08, CBOSA.

128 Compare the ruling of the SAC in Warsaw of 13.02.1997, V SA 246/96, LEX No. 31633: "when we have to do with the 'administrative discretion', duties of the authority deciding upon the evidence taking procedure are more serious than in the case of the statutory obligation of the authority".

129 Among other things, compare the ruling of the SAC in Katowice of 11.09.1996, SA/Ka 1543/95, CBOSA; ruling of the VAC in Kraków of 17.09.2013, I SA/Kr 254/13, CBOSA: "Administrative discretion is not subject to review by itself; the review covers the issue whether a decision was made in line with the basic rules of the administrative procedure and, in particular, whether it was issued on the basis of the evidence collected in the case and whether the assessment of that evidence took place in line

administrative discretion itself, it will verify the correctness of determined facts that led the body to the issue of a decision having specific contents.

It has to be reiterated that the court procedure, unlike the ordinary course of the instance, does not include repeated evidentiary proceedings and the activity of the court focuses on the verification of the correctness of findings made by the decision-making entity. It is verification through justification. This is why judicial review of the actual use of the freedom of decision by administering bodies is limited. The court verifies the compliance with the law and the correctness of actions taken and assessments made on the basis of criteria presented in the statement of reasons irrespectively of the actual motives of the body taking advantage of its freedom of decision.

The influence of rulings of administrative courts on the process of determination of facts of the case is direct and indirect at the same time. Direct influence applies to specific cases subject to the administrative court review and submitted for re-examination as a result of the repeal of an administrative decision. Such directness combines with the binding nature of findings made by the court. It results from the fact that, according to art. 153 of the Code of Administrative Courts Procedure, "the legal evaluation and indications regarding further procedure expressed in the court ruling are binding in the case for those bodies whose action, idleness or lengthy conduct of proceedings were contested and also courts unless legal regulations were changed." The judicature points out that it also covers determinations of facts in the process of the issue of administrative decisions.[130] Therefore, the administration body re-examining the case is legally obliged to consider the findings, including findings related to the facts re-examining the case. The influence of the above-mentioned regulations on the law application process will be discussed further below. In turn, the indirect influence applies to all other situations, i.e. those cases when the body intentionally or unintentionally derives knowledge of the approach of administrative courts to the determination of facts of the case, in particular, in cases with similar facts. Pragmatic reasons support the consideration of statements formulated by the court in cases other than the case subjected to the review. To avoid the repeal of their decisions in connection with the violation of legal standards and rules of law, administrative

---

with the principle of the free assessment of evidence or whether it contains elements of discretion". More related analyses can be found in chapter V.

130 The SAC ruling of 29.07.1999, IV SA 1177/97, LEX No. 47301; ruling of the SAC in Warsaw of 8.12.2005, VI SA/Wa 1052/05, LEX No. 190859, ruling of the VAC in Warsaw of 5.10.2005, VI SA/Wa 960/05, LEX No. 217347.

bodies will consider "guidelines" contained in statements of reasons in rulings of administrative courts. Therefore, the activity of the latter becomes, in fact, a "sign-post" for the administration on the one hand, having a decision-making nature (by the presentation of a method of determination of specific facts or reaching for specific evidence measures) and, on the other hand, having the nature of an argumentation (as regards related requirements resulting from the contents of legal standards and rules of law). This, in turn, leads to the conclusion that rulings of administrative courts are at the same time "motivators" for the administration as regards the need for the exhaustive determination of facts of the administrative case. The courts not only specify how the administration is supposed to determine the facts (from the procedural perspective) but also note that it has to do it in compliance with the rules previously discussed.

3.3 Validating determinations of an administrative case and judicial practice

3.3.1 Operative interpretation and the catalogue of sources of the law

Determination of the legal status of a case includes two types of actions, i.e. the choice and determination of the validity and applicability of a specific standard setting fact and the determination of its importance to a degree sufficiently precise for the needs of the settlement.[131] Depending on the legal culture and detailed systemic solutions, standard setting facts can have varied statuses and sources, and their weight as a structural component of a legal standard can vary because of that.

Therefore, two lines of reasoning appear at the stage of the ascertainment of facts in the law application process: validation reasoning (related to the search for the source of a standard) and derivative reasoning (covering the reconstruction of a standard setting statement from that source). From that perspective, there is no doubt that the "situational" nature of the law interpretation which is characteristic for processes of the issue of binding unit legal decisions (both by courts and by administration bodies). The objective of the interpretation understood in this manner and called an operative (practical) one is to issue the law application decision "adapted" to a unit case.[132] The operative interpretation

131 See J. Wróblewski, *Sądowe stosowanie prawa…*, op. cit., p. 43.

132 It was accurately stated in the ruling of the VAC in Białystok of 9.02.2012, II SA/Bk 828/11, LEX No. 1116350 – "When examining a motion in a specific case, a public administration body cannot waive its individual examination by adopting the

takes place, so to speak, on the occasion of the process leading to the issue of a decision and it would not exist without the need to issue a decision because, in principle, the interpreter is not interested in an interpretation effect other than the specification of bases for the issue of that very decision to apply the law.[133]

Operative interpretation as a part of processes of law application by decision-making entities is separable from specific features of facts of the case. From that perspective, the body obliged under a procedural order to make a decision has to determine a relevant legal basis for its issue. Therefore, it will aim at the reconstruction of that "part" of an abstractly stated legal standard necessary to it for the needs of the issue of a decision in a specific situation. In other words, the law application process does not involve the reconstruction of the "entire" legal standard because, in the light of the goal of the process (the issue of a decision in a specific situation) and its economy, the body focuses its reasoning on its fragment to which the subject of the pending case is connected.

The progress of the operative interpretation process is determined with characteristics of the case of interest to the decision-maker. Additionally, certain general "requirements" regarding the way in which such reasoning is carried out are specified in validation and derivative rules accepted in a legal order. Therefore, freedom of decision available to the decision-maker at the stage of the determination of the legal status is the resultant of the specificity of law application processes in a specific legal order. The same applies to both the range and the depth of the reconstruction of a standard.

The body applying the law aims at the reconstruction of a normative basis for a decision that will be necessary to finish the process of law application and issue a decision.[134] It is a normative complex consisting of competence, procedural and substantive components.

The adoption of a decision-making perspective of law application processes influences the catalogue of potential sources of the law the body will reach for. From that perspective, each factor influencing the contents of a legal decision will be considered a source of the law (i.e. decision-based approach to sources of the

---

automatism principle as the basis for the resolution, involving a general belief that 'each case is examined according to the same law' ".

133 See L. Leszczyński, *Wykładnia prawa – model ogólny*, [in:] *Wykładnia prawa – model ogólny a perspektywa Europejskiej Konwencji Praw Człowieka i Prawa Unii Europejskiej*, eds. A. Kalisz, L. Leszczyński, B. Liżewski, Lublin 2011, p. 15.

134 For more, see, among others: L. Leszczyński, *Wykładnia operatywna (podstawowe właściwości)*, „Państwo i Prawo" 2006, no. 6, p. 12 and consecutive pages.

law).[135] This assumption refers to the "developed normative concept of sources of the law" formulated by Z. Ziembiński that assumes that not only legal regulations but also political justifications, customs and precedents, interpretation rules and inference rules as well as rules for the settlement of collisions between standards of that system have to be classified as a part of the legal system. All of them perform the function of criteria for the classification of standards having specific contents in the system of standards in force.[136]

A look at sources of the law from the decision-making perspective makes it possible to depart (to a degree) from purely juridical categories thus expanding the scope of discretionary authority available to the body. In the statutory law culture, the adoption of a developed concept of sources of the law means that it is possible to "go beyond" the system of legal regulations and reach for other standard-creating facts as well. Additionally, the specificity of law application processes influences the range of decision-making freedom available to a body. It is because only that part of the legal order remains of interest to the decision-maker that is relevant in the light of the facts of the case. A wide approach to the construction of sources of the law assumes the possibility to reach for three basic types of sources at the stage of the search for a source of the reconstruction of a normative basis for a decision: legal regulations, other law application decisions and open criteria.[137]

The decision-making freedom available to the entity applying the law at the stage of the determination of facts of the case has to be analyzed in relation to both types of reasoning taking place within the framework of the operative interpretation, i.e. validation reasoning and derivative reasoning. It is about indicating what freedom the body has at the stage of the definition of a source of the reconstruction and the reconstruction itself of the standard to be applied. When analyzing these issues, one has to find out to what degree the decision-maker is obliged to consider specific sources in the law application process, to what degree it has freedom in this area; whether it can refuse to apply a source which validity it ascertained and, finally, how it should carry out the normative

135 More: L. Leszczyński, *Podstawa decyzji stosowania prawa administracyjnego. Ustalenia walidacyjne*, [in:] *System prawa administracyjnego, vol. 4: Wykładnia w prawie administracyjnym*, eds. R. Hauser, Z. Niewiadomski, A. Wróbel, Warszawa 2012, p. 57.

136 See S. Wronkowska, Z. Ziembiński, *Zarys teorii prawa*, op. cit., pp. 141–146. See also: J. Wróblewski, *Decyzja sądowa a koncepcja systemu prawa*, „Acta Universitatis Lodziensis, Zeszyty Naukowe UŁ Nauki Humanistyczno-Społeczne" 1978, book 28, pp. 7–8 and his concept of a "wide law system".

137 L. Leszczyński, *Podstawa decyzji stosowania prawa administracyjnego…*, op. cit., p. 58.

reconstruction process and what it can or should do in the event of an ambiguity of meaning, establishment of the existence of a conflict or a loophole in the law.

3.3.2 Influence of "precedents" on validation reasoning

The basic source of a normative basis for a decision in the continental legal culture includes legal regulations in force; at the same time, the adoption of the decision-making perspective on law application processes makes it possible to notice the influence of other facts (factors, sources) on the content of the standard to be applied. This fact influences the actual catalogue of sources of the law (standard-creating facts) the body reaches for in the process of the operative interpretation, i.e. legal regulations, other decisions (judicial and administrative precedents) as well as non-legal criteria.

The legislature has the last word on the role of each of them in the law application process as, by indicating the catalogue of sources of the law, it determines the scope of the "search" carried out by bodies applying the law. For example, the Polish Constitution of 1997 introduces a closed catalogue of sources of the law in force that, according to the legality principle, can constitute the basis for decisions of public administration bodies. In addition to national regulations (the Constitution, acts, regulations, decree-laws and ordinances), the Basic Law also includes the international law and the law established by international organizations of which the Republic of Poland is a member (laws of the European Union). The catalogue is limited to sources in the form of legal regulations contained in normative acts of varied nature and position. These regulations define the basis and the limit of activities of the administration. Additionally, sources of the law that influence the operations of the public administration also include "specific sources of the administrative law"[138] including acts of planning (e.g. local zoning plans), statutes and regulations or technical standards.

When identifying the source of legal regulations, the entity applying the law has to follow the reasoning aimed at the determination of their power in a place and at a time and their applicability. In general, the first type of reasoning refers to the thetic justification of the power of regulations, i.e. the search for an answer to the question whether a regulation was adopted according to an appropriate

138 More: J. Zimmermann, *Prawo administracyjne*, Zakamycze 2005, pp. 86–90. Compare. J. Stelmasiak, *Wybrane zagadnienia dotyczące źródeł prawa administracyjnego w świetle orzecznictwa Naczelnego Sądu Administracyjnego*, [in:] *Polski model sądownictwa administracyjnego*, eds. J. Stelmasiak, J. Niczyporuk, S. Fundowicz, Lublin 2003, pp. 312–313.

procedure and announced and whether it was repealed or amended at that point. However, the second of the above-mentioned issues entails more difficulties. When the entity applying the law states that a regulation belongs to the catalogue of sources of the law accepted by the legislator and that the regulation is in force, it will subsequently ascertain whether the regulation can be applied in the case of interest to the entity. The statement of the general applicability and possibility to apply a legal regulation as a basis for a decision combines the thetic justification with the axiological and practical one (factual, functional) referring to the specification of the way in which legal regulations thetically in force can be used as a basis for the decision to apply the law.[139]

Disregarding the possibility to reach for a precedent as a validation argument (which will be analyzed later), one has to note how other decisions to apply the law and, specifically, rulings of courts controlling the administration can influence validation findings in law application processes. Such influence is indirect and argumentative. Via the contents of their rulings, courts work out certain specific standards referring to detailed and fundamental issues connected to the reasoning mentioned above with regard to legal regulations. For the sake of clarity, a few examples can be mentioned here.

The judicature also notes that any sovereign interference of administering bodies with civic rights and freedoms is only permitted on the basis of a legislative act or an executive act issued on the basis and within the limits of an explicit authorization contained in the legislative act.[140] It means that, on the one hand, there are no grounds for the basing of a content of a decision exclusively on non-regulatory normative regulations that function within the administration. As regards the possibility of "using" the latter, the courts indicated that, even though they could not be the basis for the issue of an administrative decision, an administration body can use interpretation indications of bodies, especially central bodies, to interpret doubtful legal regulations when settling an individual administrative case.[141]

---

139 L. Leszczyński (*Podstawa decyzji stosowania prawa administracyjnego…*, op. cit., p. 67). As the author indicates, "by way of an example, it is possible to apply only provisions thetically in force while the fact of their thetic power does not cause the application of such a provision in each case".

140 Compare the ruling of the SAC in Warsaw of 6.02.1981, SA 819/80, LEX No. 9603 with the gloss of W. Dawidowicz "Orzecznictwo Sądów Polskich" 1981, no. 10, p. 189. Compare the ruling of the SAC in Warsaw of 6.02.1981, SA 819/80, LEX No. 9603.

141 The SAC ruling of 19.07.2012, I OSK 685/12, LEX No. 1217373.

Therefore, standards of the statutory rank that can constitute a validation argument by themselves or co-existing with regulations of the constitutional or lower-order rank[142] or with international or EU regulations[143] have to be the basis for all activities of administering entities. Poland's membership in the European Union is inseparably linked to the obligatory consideration of EU regulations during the reconstruction of the normative basis for a decision. This fact significantly influences both the reasoning related to the search for a source of that standards and its reconstruction.[144] Additionally, administration bodies, just like courts, are obliged to comply with the principle of supremacy of the Community law over the national law and the refusal to apply the national law non-compliant with the Community law.[145] Similar remarks are formulated with regard to the application of provisions of ratified international agreements.[146]

As regards the possibility to base an administrative decision exclusively on constitutional standards, it was stated that "a provision of the Constitution cannot be the basis for a legal administrative decision by itself".[147] Additionally, in the light of the lack of the constitutionally guaranteed independence of officials and the administration, public authorities, unlike courts, cannot refuse to apply a reconstructed statutory standard even in the event of its obvious unconstitutionality or a lower-order standard in the event of the non-compliance with provisions of the respective act.[148]

---

142 In the event of the co-existence with lower-order regulations, a statutory regulation will be, in most cases, a fundamental provision even though it does not have to be a dominating validation argument. Compare L. Leszczyński, Podstawa decyzji stosowania prawa administracyjnego…, op. cit., p. 85, 89.

143 Ruling of the SAC in Warsaw of 24.09.2001, V SA 340/01, LEX No. 80644.

144 Ruling of the VAC in Gdańsk of 19.12.2007, II SA/Gd 609/07, LEX No. 342469.

145 See the ruling of the VAC in Gliwice of 4.10.2011, I SA/Gl 761/11, LEX No. 964819. See also, among others, ruling of the VAC in Warsaw of 16.01.2012, III SA/Wa 1204/11, LEX No. 1167891.

146 See, among other things, the ruling of the VAC in Warsaw of 23.02.2009 V SA/Wa 2878/08, LEX No. 555098.

147 Ruling of the VAC in Łódź of 23.09.2009, II SA/Łd 493/09, LEX No. 580300.

148 In the SAC ruling of 16.05.2006 (I FSK 816/05, CBOSA), it stated that the "provision of art. 8.2 of the basic law does not mean that each body or entity can independently evaluate the compliance with the basic law of regulations in force and refuse to apply them if it considers them contrary to the Constitution". Compare the SAC ruling of 23.04.2009, II GSK 876/08, LEX No. 570314; the SAC ruling of 26.06.2012, II GSK 802/11, CBOSA; the SAC ruling of 13.06.2013, I OSK 15/12, LEX No. 1328347.

As regards the possibility to fill gaps in the law by way of the inference reasoning, the lack of such a possibility was decisively stressed in the case of competence standards.[149] The analysis of judicature's achievement also leads to a conclusion regarding the possibility to apply the administrative law by analogy, however, with a material limitation, i.e. that obligations cannot be imposed on an entity and its rights cannot be restricted in that manner.[150]

Finally, administrative courts often formulate important instructions related to the determination of sources of a standard or its reconstruction. For example, one can mention the specification of the issue of an "appropriate application of regulations" where the judicature worked out the established opinion that what it means in practice is the application of a regulation straightforwardly, with modifications, and also the lack of application.[151]

As we can see on the basis of the above-mentioned examples, the judicial practice of administrative courts is an important contribution to the search for the source of a standard to be applied in a specific situation by providing instructions regarding the possibility to acknowledge the power and applicability of legal regulations. Such influence is a "signpost" where (especially via established jurisprudence) administrative courts direct the reasoning of administering entities via the argumentation contained in the contents of statements of reasons and not only in cases directly subjected to judicial review.

Judicial review of the administration covers the correct selection of the catalogue of sources of the law from which the administering body interpreted standards being the basis for the initiation and execution of the process of law application and the issue of a decision ending this process as well as the correctness of the interpretative reasoning (more further in this publication). At the same time, the administrative court is not bound with the limits of the lodged complaint and it should carry out the reasoning enabling it to assess whether the decision and the process aimed at its issue comply with the legality requirement. As regards the validation findings, such reasoning will consist of the analysis of the catalogue of sources of the law that the body took or should take into account

149 Compare, among others, the CT resolution of 10.05.1994, W 7/94, LEX No. 25116.; ruling of the SAC in Łódź of 18.03.1998, II SAB/Łd 57/96, LEX No. 35140.

150 See, among other things, the ruling of the SAC in Wrocław of 7.10.1991, SA/Wr 877/91, LEX No. 10236.

151 Compare, among other things, the ruling of the SAC of 25.04.2005, OSK 1655/04, CBOSA; SAC ruling of 24.04.2007, II GSK 381/06, CBOSA; SAC ruling of 6.12.2013, II OSK 1647/12, CBOSA; decision of the SAC of 10.12.2013, II OZ 1155/13, CBOSA; SAC ruling of 13.02.2014, II FSK 956/12, CBOSA.

when determining the source of the normative basis for a decision. Depending on the characteristics of the situation, the verifying entity can have to do with a situation that is simple more complex when it comes to validation.[152] Both the selection of appropriate sources and the determination of their validity and applicability will be verified.[153]

3.3.3 A "precedent" as a source of a legal norm[154]

In principle, the use of other law application decisions ("precedents") as validation arguments occurs after appropriate legal regulations are found (and principal components of the necessary pattern of behaviour is reconstructed out of them) when such regulations are insufficient to reconstruct the standard (normative basis for a decision) necessary in the decision-making process and, in connection with that fact, they require the use of other standard-creating facts to this end, based on a general reference (e.g. art. 7 of the Code of Administrative Procedures).[155] Additionally, if non-legal factors, including prior rulings, influence the specific decision such influence can only be indirect.

For certain public administration bodies, reaching for a "precedent" could have to do with the use of (a) prior administrative decisions, i.e. the body's own decisions (especially decisions made in similar situations) or decisions made by other bodies (especially hierarchically above the body making a decision) or (b) court rulings (especially in the case of rulings referring to the activities of the body making a decision, especially in similar situations in the law application process). The administration body's reaching for a "precedent" can be the validation, derivative (reconstructive) or argumentative.

Rulings of administrative courts (both the VAC and SAC) can particularly strongly impact the law application process of the administrative type. It is noted that "public administration bodies settling similar cases and concerned about the

152 Among other things, the SAC ruling of 29.10.2007, FPS 3/07, CBOSA; SAC ruling of 6.03.2008, I OSK 314/07, CBOSA; SAC ruling of 13.05.2008, II GSK 108/08, CBOSA.

153 See, among other things, the SAC ruling of 13.12.2007, I FSK 114/07, CBOSA.

154 More: A. Szot, *„Precedens" jako pozaprzepisowa podstawa decyzji administracyjnej*, [in:] *Wykładnia operatywna prawa – perspektywa teoretyczna i dogmatyczna*, eds. L. Leszczyński, A. Szot, Toruń 2017, pub. Adam Marszałek, pp. 132–147.

155 Art. 7 of the Code of Administrative Procedures "*In the course of the procedure, public administration bodies uphold the legality; they take any action necessary to accurately clarity the facts ex officio or upon the request of the parties and to settle a case considering the social interest and the legitimate interest of citizens.*" More: L. Leszczyński, *Podstawa decyzji stosowania prawa administracyjnego…*, op. cit., p. 60.

repeal of a decision by the court treat the contents of its ruling as 'another part of the law in force' ".[156] Rulings of the EU Court of Justice and international courts, especially the European Court of Human Rights, can also indirectly influence the law application process.[157] The doctrine notes explicitly that "public administration bodies settling similar cases and concerned about the repeal of a decision by the court treat the contents of its ruling as 'another part of the law in force' ".[158]

The appearance of "precedents" in the area of interest to the public administration body from the validation perspective takes place after the initial derivative reasoning regarding the legal regulations in force and applies to those situations in which such reasoning does not allow for the reconstruction of a normative basis for a decision. In such a situation, the body obliged to examine the case and issue a settlement needs to look for a way to overcome the interpretation impasse and, if it is not possible, to finish the process with no issue of a substantive settlement.

One of the ways to counteract the normative insufficiency of the contents of legal regulations in force is to reach for prior law application decisions. Additionally, it has to be stressed decisively that "precedents" can only be an argument in the validation reasoning by way of an exception. This fact is due to the legality principle and to the need to base the contents of a decision on legal standards encoded in the standard-creating facts accepted in the specific legal system. The RP Constitution does not allow a decision modelling rights or obligations of an individual (legal entity) to be based on other decisions to apply the law. Therefore, they can become a validation argument only if there is a gap in the law, i.e. if the reconstruction of a standard from laws in force does not allow for the finalization of the decision-making process. At the same time, it can only take place to a limited degree as mentioned below in this publication.

The possibility to reach for earlier decisions to apply the law at the stage of the determination of the legal status will also depend on the type of the standard to be reconstructed that will become a normative component of the basis for the decision-making process and the final content of the decision. Therefore,

---

156 A. Błaś, J. Boć, J. Supernat, *Źródła prawa administracyjnego*, [in:] Prawo administracyjne, op. cit., p. 125.

157 Their creative nature is emphasized in the literature, treating them sometimes as a category of the "judicial law" in the form of general principles of the law – see B. Jaworska-Dębska, *Źródła prawa administracyjnego*, [in:] *Prawo administracyjne – pojęcia, instytucje, zasady w teorii i orzecznictwie*, op. cit., p. 218.

158 A. Błaś, J. Boć, J. Supernat, *Źródła prawa administracyjnego*, [in:] *Prawo administracyjne*, ed. J. Boć, Wrocław 2010, p. 125.

it depends on whether a competence standard, procedural standards or material standards (qualification standard and consequential standard) are to be determined.

The doctrine and jurisprudence stress that, in a state under the rule of law, only a statutory act can be a source of the competence standard offering the right to issue a sovereign settlement for an entity, that unilaterally models its rights or obligations and the existence of competencies cannot be presumed.[159] As indicated in jurisprudence: "free interpretation and adoption, as its result, of an extensive interpretation in the case of a competence standard could cause an abuse in the application of the law".[160] However, it is worth remembering that one cannot presume that part of the competence that entails the right to act, which is permitted with regard to the presumption of an existence of the obligation to make use of that right. Such an obligation can result from the contents of tasks standards and their realization can actually be determined, to a degree, by decisions made by other public administration bodies.

Equivalent remarks regarding the need for the existence of statutory bases have to be formulated with regard to the reconstruction of substantive standards. The legal basis for each administrative decision regardless of its addressee, both imposing obligations and granting rights, can only consist of legal regulations in force.[161] For that group of standards, reaching for a precedent can apply at most

---

159 As, among others, J. Zimmermann, *Prawo administracyjne…*, op. cit., p. 120 and W. Jakimowicz, *Wykładnia w prawie administracyjnym*, Warszawa 2006, p. 458, P. Czarny, *Trybunał Konstytucyjny a wykładnia ustaw w zgodzie z Konstytucją*, [in:] *Polska kultura prawna a proces integracji europejskiej*, ed. S. Wronkowska, Kraków 2005, p. 88; J. Zimmermann, *Aksjomaty prawa administracyjnego*, Warszawa 2013, pp. 168–169; W. Jakimowicz, *Konstrukcja tzw. domniemania kompetencji organu administracji publicznej*, [in:] *Nowe problemy badawcze w teorii prawa administracyjnego*, eds. J. Boć, A. Chajbowicz, Wrocław 2009. See, among other things, the SAC resolution of 15.12.2004, FPS 2/04, LEX No. 137421; SC resolution of 22.04.1997, III ZP 1/97, LEX No. 30547. CT resolution of 10.05.1994, W 7/94, LEX No. 25116; SC resolution of 22.04.1997, III ZP 1/97, LEX No. 30547, SC resolution of 22.04.1997, III ZP 1/97, LEX No. 30547.

160 Ruling of the VAC in Lublin of 18.09.2008, II SA/Lu 453/08, LEX No. 516108.

161 See the ruling of the SAC in Warsaw of 20.07.1981, SA 805/81, LEX No. 9631. "Administrative decisions can only be issued on the basis of the law in force" – ruling of the SAC in Kraków of 20.02.1994, SA/Kr 1428/93, LEX No. 24499. Compare the ruling of the SAC in Warsaw of 27.04.1981, SA 767/81, LEX No. 9616; ruling of the SAC in Warsaw of 25.03.1981, SA 353/81, LEX No. 9612.

to technical cases or cases of lower importance that are frequently changed and can only supplement legal regulations in force.

In turn, "precedents" can have an interesting influence on the modelling of the decision-making practice of a specific body that is identified in the doctrine of the administrative law with the custom understood as the "non-legal habitual conduct complied with practically within an organizational structure of the administration, in similar situations and at a specific time".[162] This topic will be discussed in greater detail in the next chapter.

3.4 Determination of the content of a legal norm

3.4.1 The influence of jurisprudence on the interpretation

Derivative reasoning being a part of the operative interpretation of the law leads to the reconstruction of a normative basis for a decision from specific standard-creating facts that became of interest to the decision-maker for validation purposes. The entity applying the law will carry out such reasoning using specific interpretation rules acceptable in the given legal order for that purpose. In each law application process, the decision-maker can take advantage of all principles of law interpretation and is not limited in that area in any way. Therefore, the freedom of decision regarding their selection is unlimited in a sense. Another manifestation of the discretionary power of the administration in the context of interpretation processes consists of the possibility to depart from the linguistic formulation of a regulation if the use of non-linguistic rules fails to confirm the results of the linguistic interpretation. This fact will cause an additional reflection of the entity applying the law. It will have to answer the question about the meaning of results of the non-linguistic interpretation, in particular, whether an adjustment of the linguistic reading of the standard from the legal regulation and, in an extreme case, the complete departure from it is possible and necessary. Discretionary power of administration bodies at the derivation stage manifests particularly strongly in the possibility to depart from the significance of a standard interpreted with the use of linguistic rules for the benefit of its narrower (*interpretatio restrictiva*) or wider (*interpretatio extensiva*) understanding. However, this possibility becomes the body's duty in certain cases and, in that sense, has a limiting impact on its freedom of decision. It happens, for example, when results of the linguistic interpretation lead to absurd results.[163]

162 More: A. Błaś, J. Boć, J. Supernat, *Źródła prawa administracyjnego*, op. cit., pp. 121–124.
163 Compare the resolution of the SAC in Warsaw of 25.06.2001, FPS 7/00, CBOSA; SAC ruling of 8.11.2007, II OSK 1474/06, CBOSA.

An interesting manifestation of that duty and its consequences can be seen in the SAC of 13.08.2008[164] in which the court considered it necessary to depart from the literal meaning of the definition contained in the law.

However, it has to be remembered that the obligatory linguistic interpretation should be complied with particularly restrictively in all those cases when the protection of the citizens' sense of safety is required as they should not be surprised with an extension or restriction of the meaning of legal provisions when they act trusting them.[165] This is why the possibility to depart from the *interpretatio declarativa* should be additionally assessed considering the type of the interpreted standard.

Law interpretation in the administrative type of law application seems to be more determined with the variety of conditions in which administering entities operate than in the case of the judicial type. This situation results from the organizational and political entanglement, and also from the very essence of activities of the public administration in a state. Therefore, juridical, political, social, praxeological and ethical considerations influence law application processes including law interpretation and the attainment of the goal and functions of the administrative law require the undermining of the rank of protected goods and the consideration of varied rationales and phenomena.[166]

The influence of rulings of administrative courts on the law interpretation process is argumentative – as courts indicate their approach to interpretation processes or their execution through theses formulated in statements of reasons for the rulings or explicitly show the way they understand a legal standard – while they also provide the direct or indirect influence. This fact results from the specificity of the process comprising the verification of the correctness of interpretation reasoning. Both the instance control and judicial review can be reduced to a similar reasoning scheme. It is about the confrontation and comparison of results of the interpretation made by a body with a specific template, i.e. interpretation results received by the entity executing the verification.

---

164 More: SAC ruling of 13.08.2008, I OSK 1080/07, LEX No. 516786: "[…] rules of the systemic and purposive interpretation when determining the understanding of that provision indicate the need to depart, for the use of the analyzed regulation, from the strict understanding of that phrase compliant with the literal phrasing of the statutory definition, which is insufficient in this case".

165 See: L. Morawski, *Zasady wykładni prawa*, Toruń 2006, p. 196.

166 More: Z. Duniewska, *Wybrane aspekty wykładni prawa administracyjnego (racje i właściwości)*, [in:] *Koncepcja systemu prawa administracyjnego*, ed. J. Zimmermann, Warszawa 2007, pp. 667–668.

Such confrontation leads to a conclusion regarding the compliance or divergence of these two components and the conclusion involves the evaluation of the correctness of the validation and derivation findings. In particular, verifying bodies determine the correctness of the interpretation result itself, i.e. the "contents" of the normative basis for a decision. They can only indirectly analyse the correctness of the method of its attainment, i.e. the reasoning carried out to reconstruct the standard to be applied from specific standard-creating facts. In practice, the verification refers to those arguments that were externalized in the statement of reasons for a decision. According to art. 107 of the Polish Code of Administrative Procedures, the content of an administrative decision should contain, among other things, an indication of the legal basis for an action and the statement of legal reasons. It entails the need to refer to the content of legal regulations in a decision and "explain their meaning" to the addressee. The verification of the reasoning aimed at the determination of the legal background of the case consists of the verification of the statement of the law with regard to the determination of the authority of the body to resolve the case, procedural actions to be taken in the course of the process as well as material aspects of the process and the final decision.

In addition to the verification of the correct selection of the source of the normative basis for a decision, the scope of the control of determination of the legal status also covers the verification of the correctness of determination of its contents. It means that the reconstruction process and its final effect in the form of a standard to be applied will be controlled by the administrative court. Therefore, it is necessary to determine during that process whether the administration body used possible interpretation rules correctly. Depending on the catalogue of sources of the law defined as a result of the validation reasoning, sub-branches of the administrative law[167] and facts of the case, the importance of individual interpretation rules will vary.

Theoretical assumptions underlying the interpretation by the verifying entity can also be varied. If the principle of subsidiarity of non-linguistic interpretation rules[168] is adopted the entity can consider that, in that case, reaching for such

167 Compare, among others, the SAC ruling of 25.06.2008, II FSK 626/07, CBOSA; SAC ruling of 29.07.2008, II FSK 717/07, CBOSA; SAC ruling of 29.07.2008, II FSK 1606/07, LEX No. 486477.

168 As, among other things, in the SAC ruling of 21.08.2008, II OSK 937/07, LEX No. 488291; SAC decision of 25.11.2008, II GZ 299/08, CBOSA; SAC ruling of 30.05.2008, I GSK 697/07, CBOSA.

rules was neither necessary nor justified due to the linguistic explicitness of the regulation and, as a consequence, can undermine the related reasoning of the administering entity. In turn, the verification process will be different (from the argumentation perspective) if the verifying entity adopts the completeness principle in the law interpretation process.[169]

In the light of the fact that administration bodies create rights and obligations of individual entities by way of administration acts, the judicial review of the correctness of the interpretation of legal regulations including lower-order regulations cannot be overestimated despite the general cassation competence of such courts. Additionally, the lack of uniformity of the judicature itself, both as regards instructions and guidelines related to the execution of interpretation processes and methods of "understanding" of specific legal standards is an observable system weakness. In practice, it can result in the body, knowing two different (sometimes colliding) ruling practices of administrative courts as regards the interpretation of regulations being the basis for the projected administrative decision, being forced to select one of them and, at the same time, taking into account potential consequences of repeal of the decision. Such a situation does not positively influence the strengthening of the principle of legal certainty and predictability of its application.

The influence of judicial and administrative rulings on interpretation processes executed by public administration bodies can also take on a direct and decision-making form. It happens with regard to the said art. 153 of the Code of Administrative Courts Procedure. That regulation is mandatory, which means that both the public administration body and the court re-examining the case cannot fail to take into account the legal assessment and indications previously expressed in the court ruling because they are bound with them. The failure to comply with that regulation would, in essence, undermine the principle of judicial review of files and activities of administration bodies in force in a democratic state under the rule of law and would lead to the inconsistency in the operation of the public authority system. Being bound with the legal assessment expressed in a ruling and the resulting indications regarding further procedure means that the formulation of new legal assessments expressed in a court ruling by the administration body whose decision was subjected to judicial review is ruled out. The body is obliged to submit to the ruling completely and consistently react if non-compliance with the indications regarding further procedure

169 See the SAC ruling of 27.11.2007, I OSK 695/07, CBOSA.

in the public administration body is found out.[170] This is why art. 153 of the Code of Administrative Courts Procedure defines a relationship between the administrative body and the court that can be reduced to the body being bound with the legal assessment and indications of further procedure, where there is no space for the body's polemics with the legal assessment and indications of further procedure.[171] Jurisprudence of the Supreme Administrative Court emphasizes that the obligation to comply with the legal assessment expressed in the ruling of an administrative court imposed both on the body and on the court can only be exempted in the event of a material change of the legal status or facts, making the legal opinion outdated and also if the ruling is challenged in the mode provided for under the law.[172]

The indicated legal assessment entails, in particular, a specific interpretation of provisions of the substantive and procedural law and aims at the clarification of the material content of legal regulations and their application in a specific case in connection with the case being examined. Indications regarding further procedure are, as a rule, consequences of the legal assessment and refer to the behaviour during the re-examination of the case. Additionally, they aim to help prevent errors already made and to indicate the direction of future procedures in order to avoid further or other defects or breaches of procedure. Therefore, whenever a case is examined, bodies will be bound with the legal assessment conducted by the court for as long as the ruling expressing it is not repealed or for as long as the regulations in force are not materially changed.[173] It is also worth noting that provisions of art. 153 of the Code of Administrative Courts Procedure mean that the court ruling covers the future administrative procedure regarding the same case.[174] One cannot ignore here the importance of the second institution regulated under art. 153 of the Code of Administrative Courts Procedure, i.e. indications of further procedure that, as a rule, are a consequence of the legal assessment contained in the cassation ruling issued by the court. Such indications refer to the behaviour in the course of the re-examination of the case; their aim is to avoid and eliminate errors previously made and to specify

170 See the SAC ruling of 30.07.2009, II FSK 451/08, CBOSA; SAC ruling of 23.09.2009, I FSK 494/09, CBOSA; SAC ruling of 13.07.2010, I GSK 940/09, CBOSA; ruling of the VAC in Wrocław of 14.01.2010, I SA/Wr 1591/09, CBOSA.

171 See the ruling of the VAC in Poznań of 27.11.2013, IV SA/Po 537/13, CBOSA.

172 See the SAC ruling of 26.06.2000, I SA/Ka 2408/98, CBOSA; ruling of the VAC in Opole of 3.07.2012, II SA/Op 239/12, CBOSA.

173 Ruling of the SAC in Warsaw of 6.02.2013, II GSK 2101/11, CBOSA.

174 Compare the ruling of the SAC in Warsaw of 14.03.2013, I GSK 1591/11, CBOSA.

the direction the future procedure should take to avoid defects involving deficiencies in the procedural material or violations of procedural regulations.

The legal assessment expressed in the court ruling is a manifestation of the judicial law created via the rulings of administrative courts interpreting standards of the administrative law and also demonstrating what standards are to be used in a specific case and how. It is true that courts are not, in principle, authorized to issue substantive settlements; however, their interpretation occurs for the needs of the review of settlements contested in them. Therefore, they secondarily formulate standards of the second degree and, with their use, model the future judicial practice and the way in which public administration bodies settle cases.

3.4.2 "Contents" of general reference clauses

In order to enable the adaptation of the contents of projected legal decisions to the rapidly changing reality, the legislature introduces structures supposed to make law application processes more flexible to the legal system. Such structures are manifestations of the intended freedom of decision described in chapter I. They include, among others, general reference clauses and indeterminate phrases. Their "contents" are subject to determination every time in the law application process. Such contents are related both to structures referring to specific features of specific situations (e.g. "individual interest") and also to systemic clauses (e.g. "public interest"). However, their occurrence in the system does not entail the decision-makers arbitrariness. The decision-maker has to determine their contents in the context of specific facts of the case, considering rules and principles of the legal system[175] and the entirety of social values (non-legal). For example, when the general clause structure refers to certain values, standards and assessments beyond the law system, it does not mean that the body applying the law is granted the unlimited possibility to "model" their contents, especially when confronted with certain values established in a democratic state under the rule of law.

Few attempts at the *in abstracto* "definition" of systemic general clauses were made in the judicature in the past. Examples include an attempt to determine the understanding of the "public interest" structure in the SC ruling of 31.05.1933.[176]

175 See Z. Janowicz, *Kodeks postepowania administracyjnego. Komentarz*, Warszawa 1999, p. 602.

176 An "interest" is either the existing or future material or personal asset, or an ideal asset related to the organization of the communal life and the correctness of its functionality. A "public" interest is a collective interest of a social organization, state or a local government, or social life in general – see the SC ruling of 31.05.1933, II K 285/33.

However, such attempts have been abandoned for the benefit of the *in concreto* "definition" of clauses, i.e. in reference to specific characteristics of the actual situation. At the same time, it could seem that, in the light of the role of entities applying the law when determining the contents of references, decision-makers (courts, public administration bodies) will make attempts at indicating specific values underlying a clause. Going further, one could argue that decision-making processes contribute to a certain universalization of values. If one assumes that authorized bodies reviewing decisions including, e.g. a general reference clause as a component of the normative basis, influence their understanding by lower-instance bodies they also influence (at least indirectly) the contents of future decisions to apply the law. However, this assumption is not confirmed (at least sufficiently) by practice. The practice of law application most frequently goes in the direction of the general referencing in the statement of reasons for a decision of a specific clause that the decision-maker was obliged to use with no more specific definition of how the body (the court, administration body) understood it or to specify it on an example (usually in the context of specific facts).[177]

However, it does not mean that court rulings fail to influence the practical understanding and use of specific general clauses. Due to their authority and importance, courts define certain, even if general, directions in that area. For example, the evolution of the perception and definition of relations between the clauses of the "social interest" and "legitimate interest of citizens" pursuant to art. 7 of the Polish Code of Administrative Procedures is worth mentioning.[178] Both these structures and also their mutual relations significantly depend on the axiology prevailing at a given moment of the historical development of the society and also on the prevailing ideology due to their non-legal entanglement.

177 See, among others, the SAC ruling of 22.04.1999 r., SA/Sz 850/98, LEX No. 36843; ruling of the VAC in Lublin of 15.03.2013 r., I SA/Lu 612/12; SAC ruling of 5.04.2001, II SA 725/00, LEX No. 53476.

178 For more, compare M. Wyrzykowski, *Pojęcie interesu społecznego w prawie administracyjnym*, Warszawa 1986, p. 52; W. Jakimowicz, *Wykładnia w prawie administracyjnym*, op. cit., pp. 124–125, A. Żurawik, *„Interes publiczny", „interes społeczny" i „interes społecznie uzasadniony"*, „Ruch Prawniczy, Ekonomiczny i Socjologiczny" 2003, book. 2, pp. 60–62; ruling of the VAC in Gliwice of 7.02.2013, IV SA/Gl 211/12, LEX No. 1278056; SAC ruling of 26.07.2006, II OSK 1004/05, LEX No. 266429; ruling of the SAC in Warsaw of 24.05.1999, II SA 547/99, LEX No. 46292; SAC ruling of 7.12.2011, I OSK 4/11, LEX No. 1149372; ruling of the SAC in Warsaw of 11.06.1981, SA 820/81, LEX No. 9626; SC ruling of 18.11.1993, III ARN 49/93, LEX No. 9595; CT ruling of 20.03.2006, K 17/05, LEX No. 182494;

This phenomenon is particularly vivid in changes of the ruling practice from the period of the real socialism Poland when the social interest was identified with the interest of an individual and their potential conflict was settled for the benefit of the former[179] to contemporary times (after 1989) when the balance of such interests is highlighted along with the need to weigh them every time in the event of a collision with no *a priori* assumptions regarding the supremacy of any of them. The beginning of the related change can be traced back to the above-mentioned ruling of the SAC in Warsaw of 11.06.1981 even though its content contains the reference to the supremacy of the social interest in a socialist state.[180]

The analysis of the ruling practice of administrative courts indicates that they are relatively unwilling to carry out in-depth deliberations on the contents of general reference clauses. In addition to the above-mentioned examples of their "defining" or attempts to specify mutual relations between specific clauses, it is difficult to find related "guidelines" for administration bodies in statements of reasons for rulings. At the same time, those attempts that are made transform, in principle, into more or less established ruling practice. It leads to a conclusion regarding a rather general impact of rulings issued by administrative courts that direct administering bodies regarding the approach to the determination of contents of general reference clauses.

3.4.3 Pragmatic arguments for the consideration of rulings of administrative courts

Opinions expressed in court rulings as regards law interpretation and conduct become the basic instrument modelling the ruling practice of public administration bodies. Being bound with a court interpretation, which takes place pursuant to the said art. 153 of the Code of Administrative Courts Procedure, does not only apply to a court and a public administration body whose action or idleness were covered in a court procedure but also covers any other body taking part in a procedure conducted within the limits of a case if the court ruling covered acts or activities preceding an act or an activity being the subject of a complaint. It means that a ruling of an administrative court has effects going beyond the scope of administrative court proceedings. A pragmatic approach to rules modelled in the ruling practice and interpretation theses makes it possible for a body

179 Compare, among other things, the ruling of the SAC in Warsaw of 4.06.1982, I SA 255/82, LEX No. 11293; ruling of the SAC in Warsaw of 5.11.1981, I SA 2178/81, LEX No. 11254.

180 See also the ruling of the SAC in Warsaw of 25.11.1988, IV SA 540/88, LEX No. 10029.

to avoid defects in the administrative procedure and administrative acts issued as its result. It is obvious that, if an administration body has a ruling in which an opinion was expressed in a case of interest to it the use of theses contained there will be highly likely in situations and examined cases equivalent to the evaluated one. The application of a different conduct not only seems to make no sense but is also pointless. If a court ruling is based on an interpretation already established in the judiciary (courts of the same and higher instance) its duplication in similar cases will be more likely. If an opinion of the court is known one can expect it to be applied and disseminated by other juries. One cannot help but have an impression that a court, by its very nature, will take advantage of its existing ruling practice to the same degree as an administration body. Of course, a departure of the common, established ruling practice is possible but such a situation is rather exceptional.

The body's compliance with opinions resulting from the established ruling practice of administrative courts also makes it possible to avoid potential sanctions in the form of a repeal of an administrative decision issued in a similar situation. It would be completely pointless to "reinvent the wheel" in the interpretation process and model it anew in the light of the fact that the court has already completed that process. Therefore, if a ready-made interpretation is available it will be obvious to take advantage of judicial achievements and create an administrative achievement. The same facts determine the willingness to avoid obvious judicial sanctions due to the undermining of administrative decisions and judicial costs generated as a result. Statistics related to the elimination of administrative acts from the judiciary as a result of judicial review also model the assessment of the effectiveness and efficiency of the administration and contribute to the lawfulness and general social approval of the public administration activities.

The ruling practice of administration bodies shows that the above-mentioned activity of administration bodies is a common phenomenon. For example, the practice related to the application of an administrative monetary penalty after the repeal of provisions of the act on environmental protection in the ruling issued by the Constitutional Tribunal[181] in which, despite the actual postponement of the date of the entry into force of the constitutional tribunal's decision until art. 88 of the act on environmental protection has been amended, administrative courts and, after that, public administration bodies of both instances complied with the opinion expressed there. As a result, a certain practice emerged, modelled with

181 CT ruling of 1.07.2014, SK 6/12, OTK-A 2014/7/68, Dz. U. 2014 item 926.

the judicial ruling practice as a result of which administration bodies not only failed to apply the sanction contained in the said provision but also considered the binding nature of the judicial interpretation for administration bodies.[182] The Tribunal's ruling was not yet final because, as mentioned above, the Tribunal decided to postpone the expiry of unconstitutional provisions; however, the position taken by the Tribunal and administrative courts making decisions after its issue and the assessment expressed there, confirming the non-compliance with the Constitution of legal regulations being the basis for the issue of the contested decision determined the elimination of decisions based on provisions not compliant with the indicated provisions of the Constitution. The above-mentioned example evidently shows the modelling of the ruling practice of administration bodies on the basis of the judicial practice and this is not a one-time case.

Therefore, the current ruling practice, especially in administration bodies of the higher instance, does not involve the examination of a case in the course of the appeal procedure with the omission of the ruling practice of administrative courts. The prior search for court rulings issued in equivalent, similar situations is a material component of the reasoning of such bodies. It makes it possible to build both the sentence of the law application act and its statement of reasons on the basis of current theses and opinions created by courts. In this manner, the principle of persuasion resulting from art. 11 of the Code of Administrative Procedures and also the principle of promotion of citizen confidence under art. 8 § 1 of the Code of Administrative Procedures are complied with. It should be noted that the current regulation of the code of administrative procedures also orders, in art. 8 § 2 of the Code of Administrative Procedures that public administration bodies should not depart from the established case settlement practice in the same situations and legal statuses with no justified reason. Therefore, the ruling identity of appeal bodies themselves is modelled on the basis of the established judicial practice.

A few conclusions result from the above-mentioned facts. In particular, one cannot help but notice the role of the judicial ruling practice in the modelling of opinions expressed in law application acts of administration bodies in the contemporary operation of the public administration. The judicial ruling practice clearly and often directly determines the contents of statements of reasons of administration bodies of both instances. Another observable practice is that, in the event of a collision of standards in most cases (which results from the analysis

182 Compare the ruling of the VAC in Lublin of 30.09.2014, II SA/Lu 717/14, CBOSA; ruling of the SAC in Warsaw of 4 December 2014, II OSK 2697/14, CBOSA.

of the ruling practice of boards) where there is a conflict between the judicial argumentation and the initial interpretation made by the body, the former was given precedence, in particular, as a result of the pragmatism and procedural economy mentioned above as well as the willingness for the body to avoid potential sanctions in the form of the cassation ruling issued by the court, additionally entailing financial sanctions. The use of the ruling practice has an additional advantage of a rather widespread borrowing of interpretation arguments and helps solve legal problems resulting from difficulties in the interpretation of legal regulations that are often rather unclear (or even enigmatic). Using the judicial ruling practice in the manner described above starts to resemble their treatment as precedents on the basis of which the contents of issued administrative acts is generated. That process is manifested in the said, more and more frequent, reaching for judicial rulings as the basis for the generation of contents of administrative decisions. Therefore, the existing practice observed in the case of judicial authorities involving the construction of settlements on the basis of opinions presented earlier starts to be taken over by public administration bodies in the administrative type of law application. It is one of the components of the construction of the principle of trust in state bodies as a justified right of a citizen to expect a certain action of the state, predictability and consequences of action taken by its bodies.

3.5 Influence of jurisprudence on content of administrative decision

3.5.1 Bound administrative decisions

The influence of court rulings on the content of the final decision varies depending on the freedom available to the public administration body at that stage of the law application process. With some simplification, such situations in general can be divided into two main groups: (1) situations involving the legal determination of the contents of the settlement and (2) situations in which a decision is made on the basis of the administrative discretion structure. In other words, these are cases in which, on the one hand, the ascertainment of specific facts of the case by the body results in the issue of a single-content decision and, on the other hand, the legislature leaves a certain freedom of decision in the form of the possibility to choose alternative contents of the final decision.[183]

---

183 More: J. Wróblewski, *Sądowe stosowanie prawa*, op. cit., pp. 240–242.

The former situation arises if consequences of the occurrence of facts of the case are determined in an unambiguous, categorical and unconditional manner. In such a situation, the decision-maker has no possibility of evaluation of the grounds for the issue of a decision with the defined content. In such a situation, if the legal standard unambiguously determines legal consequences of a fact the resolution of the case is fully determined by that standard. Such situations are called "constrained decisions" in contrast to decisions with regard to which the body has a certain degree of discretion.

However, it has to be remembered that this legal solution or, in other words: the lack of freedom of decision, refers to the last stage of the decision-making process, i.e. the issue of the final decision. If we look at this problem from the perspective of the entire law application process and manifestations of discretionary power being a part of various types of reasoning occurring at different stages of that process we can pose a hypothesis that there are no completely constrained decisions; there are only decisions with regard to which a body has a certain degree of freedom that becomes completely reduced at the stage of the formulation of legal consequences. The adoption of a different assumption would entail the rejection of the concept of existence of any freedoms of decision in the law application process, which is not true in the light of analyses already conducted. Therefore, the "constrained decision" term has to be referred to the last stage of the law application process assuming that the use of that term does not negate the possibility of occurrence of various manifestation of the body's discretionary power at other stages of the process.

In the case of "constrained decisions", the body's activity is "constrained" at the decision issue stage to the technical activity involving the individualization of a general legal standard. However, it is worth stressing that this situation does not mean that the body acts automatically and does not rule out the possibility of an occurrence of the freedom of decision at the stage involving the determination of facts, legal status or their qualification and the construction of the statement of reasons.

In the case of constrained decisions, the scope of review of the administrative court is limited to the statement whether the contents of the body's settlement comply with the legal standard categorically specifying legal consequences of specific facts. Therefore, it is possible to conclude with some simplification that this is a zero-one verification, i.e. either the contents of a decision are "within" the limits of a legal standard or not. As we can see, the ruling practice of administrative courts plays the role of a "brake" in the case of such decisions and its influence is a direct and decision-making one. Of course, arguments used by the court in the statement of reasons for a ruling are important from the perspective of the body noticing mistakes it has made; however the judicial settlement by itself determines the future reasoning of the administration body, both in the same and in other case (especially in similar situations).

Additionally, one should consider potential reasons for the body to make a decision non-compliant with the standard unambiguously specifying legal consequences. At least three such reasons can be observed: (1) a mistake made by the body in connection with an improper interpretation of a consequential standard (determining legal consequences of specific facts); (2) an error related to an incorrect qualification of facts of the case; (3) a body making a conscious decision resulting in the *contra legem* settlement, e.g. under the influence of an impulse coming from beyond the administration (external guidelines) or from the centre of the political authority.

The first group of situations involves, in principle, an incorrect interpretation and entails the possibilities of verification of such a situation by the course as described in previous subchapters. The third of the situations listed above will be discussed in greater detail in the next chapter. Therefore, the second situation, i.e. incorrect qualification is worth discussing here.

The qualification involves checking whether both factual backgrounds, i.e. the factual background of the case and an abstract background covered in the standard overlap. From the theoretical perspective, such a check requires the "translation" between "languages": from the language of the evidence to the legal language and vice versa, which can often entail significant difficulties. For example, such difficulties can result from the method of creation of legal regulations and edition of the legal text when the legislature departs from the creation of legal definitions or uses imprecise phrases. An imprecise specification of concepts related to facts of the case in a legal standard, frequently expressed in an assessing manner entails the granting of a certain discretionary power to the body applying the law in connection with their qualification.

One should also remember that the qualification takes place simultaneously with the interpretation process and the reductive reasoning being its part. Therefore, both the qualification standard and the consequential standard are gradually reduced at the stage of the determination of facts of the case. However, their final shape in that part that will make them a component of the normative basis for a decision will be "achieved" only after the qualification reasoning. Therefore, the qualification reasoning is subjected to a particular analysis by administrative course in each case and especially in the case of constrained decisions, being one of the possible (in the event of an incorrect qualification) reasons for the making of an administrative decision non-compliant with the law. However, this fact does not change the influence of the jurisprudence on activities of the administration as mentioned above. A minor remark can be mentioned with regard to situations in which the course lists more accurately the errors made by a body at the qualification stage. In that situation, the argumentative layer of the ruling can influence the future behaviour of the administering entity as regard the qualification of facts of the case from the perspective of the criteria specified in the legal standard.

The directness of the influence of the ruling practice of administrative courts on constrained decisions, in certain situations, can be combined with the legal constraint and even with the possibility to "replace" an administrative decision with a court ruling. In 2015, the Polish legislature introduced the provision of art. 145a of the Code of Administrative Courts Procedure to the legal system, according to which (in strictly specified cases) the court "puts the body under the obligation to issue a decision or a ruling within the specified time, indicating the method of case resolution or its settlement". This obligation entails the sanction in the form of a fine for the body. Additionally, in the event of the failure to comply with that obligation, the court can issue a related ruling. At the same time, it is worth noting that the above-mentioned competence of the court does not apply to decisions issued by public administration bodies as a part of the administrative discretion.

The term "indicating the method of case resolution" used in art. 145 of the Code of Administrative Courts Procedure includes the expression of legal opinions related to the substantive law which consideration would determine a specific method of the substantive settlement of a case, including the inclusion of substantive instructions determining the method of case resolution by an administration body by way of deciding upon the reasonableness or the lack of reasonableness of the application of certain regulations; inclusion in the ruling of instructions determining the content of a decision, including by way of the statement concerning merits of the case and also the specification of the method of taking evidence regarding the existence of specific facts and circumstances; evaluation of evidence indicated in the case or determination of facts on the basis of the evidence already collected in the case file. In turn, the "method of case settlement" can involve the explicit specification of the content of a decision to be issued by the body after the ruling of an administrative court becomes final or determining the content of the case settlement by an appeal authority by way of the order to consider or not to consider motions of the appellant.

The regulation mentioned above is supposed to prevent cases in which court guidelines are not implemented. However, it has to be stressed decisively that the settlement based on art. 145a § 1 of the Code of Administrative Courts Procedure is not an administrative decision. Therefore, the judicial competence granted to administrative courts does not entail the general competence standard equipping them, to the simultaneous exclusion of public administration bodies, with the right to an authoritative specification of standards of the substantive administrative law that would involve a transformation of the contents of general abstract statutory standards into a specific-individual standard such as an administrative decision.

3.5.2 Administrative discretion

The situation in which a body has freedom of decision at the last stage of the law application process applies to all those cases when the legal standard grants a certain degree of freedom to the decision-maker, involving the possibility to choose from among various consequences. Therefore, it has to do with all those situations in which the legislature introduced the "administrative discretion" structure to the legal system. In such cases, the body that has qualified the facts and the legal situation has the right to decide upon the consequences chosen from among types of consequences specified in the legal standard. It means that it can choose a solution that is optimal from the perspective of the adopted criteria.[184] From the chronological perspective, this selection takes place in the final phases of the decision-making process.[185]

One can add as a side note that administrative discretion cannot be identified with each manifestation of the freedom of decision in the law application process mentioned in previous parts of this publication. In particular, it cannot be identified with the interpretation of indeterminate phrases or general reference clauses. It is true that their occurrence in a legal text offers a degree of freedom of decision to the body; however, it is not a basis for the discretionary nature of a decision in the sense of the selection of a resolution.[186] The interpretation of ambiguous concepts entails the need for an interpretation of such a concept, which takes place at earlier stages of the law application process. However, the fact that such activities occur in various phases of the decision-making process does not mean that they are not interrelated. The formula authorizing administrative discretion is frequently supplemented with conditions specified in the form of ambiguous phrases and their realization is practically dependent on the interpretation. It is even possible for the restriction of administrative

---

184 Compare the ruling of the VAC in Wrocław of 30.01.1996, SA/Wr 3095/95, LEX No. 26643.

185 Compare the ruling of the VAC in Rzeszów of 16.12.2010, I SA/Rz 715/10, CBOSA.

186 Compare the SAC ruling of 21.10.2010, I OSK 827/10, LEX No. 602347.

discretion due to the use of such concepts of clauses to occur. From that perspective, e.g. references from art. 7 of the Code of Administrative Procedures direct the reasoning of the administration body making decisions within the limits of administrative discretion. It means that discretionary power of the administration manifested as the possibility to choose one of the legally permitted settlements as a part of the administrative discretion is directed via the need to determine the contents of both clauses contained in that regulation and their weighing in the context of a specific situation. Therefore, it becomes the directive of the choice of consequences.[187]

Administrative discretion does not allow the body freedom of action or freedom of the selection of any consequences. The scope of freedom available to the body is limited by general rules of administrative procedure. An administration body operating within the limits of discretion is obliged to take said rules into account throughout the proceedings (i.e. also when selecting consequences). The judicial review of the administration body's discretion is limited to the statement whether the limits of such discretion expressed, among other things, in values reflected in general rules of the Code of Administrative Procedures have been violated. Any violation of such rules needs to have clear signs based on the evidence collected in the case. Otherwise, the body would be devoid of the right to make a choice, which is inseparably linked to the discretion.[188]

The fact that a decision is based on a standard authorizing the administrative discretion does not rule out the possibility of verification of the legality of an administrative act; however, it entails the limitation of its scope. If such a standard grants the possibility to choose legal consequences to the entity then each choice within the limits of its discretion is legal and cannot be undermined by the court. The court examines the decision's compliance with the law but does not examine its validity or efficacy.[189] Therefore, the control over such decisions does not involve the examination of the content of the resolution itself but rather of the way in which the body reached a specific resolution and whether that resolution is "within the limits" defined by the law. Firstly, it involves checking whether the issue of a decision was preceded by a correctly executed procedure subject to detailed procedural standard and general rules of conduct.[190] In

187 Compare, among other things, the SAC ruling of 19.06.2013, II GSK 319/12, CBOSA; ruling of the VAC in Warsaw of 17.06.2013, VI SA/Wa 959/13, CBOSA; ruling of the VAC in Warsaw of 25.06.2012, VI SA/Wa 268/12, CBOSA.

188 Ruling of the SAC in Łódź of 7.02.1996, SA/Łd 917/95, LEX No. 26695.

189 See the SAC ruling of 10.07.2009, I OSK 1293/08, CBOSA.

190 See the ruling of the SAC in Katowice of 11.09.1996, SA/Ka 1543/95, CBOSA.

particular, the court verifies whether all steps necessary to accurately clarify the facts were taken during the procedure. To this end, the method of collection and evaluation of all facts material for the case is verified. The court should also accurately check the method of determination of the legal status by the body. When doing that, the court cannot limit itself to the acknowledgement of existence of the legal basis for the issue of a decision; it should also check whether the body considered all regulations potentially applicable to the case.[191]

The statement of reasons is a component of the decision based on administrative discretion that should be analyzed in depth by the administrative court. A correctly constructed statement of reasons makes it possible to check whether the administrative body executed the procedure correctly (correctly determined the factual and legal background). However, its control should not be limited to checking whether the statement of reasons contains all the components specified in the regulations ("surface structure"); it should also verify whether the statement of reasons follows the principle of persuasion and the principle of promotion of the citizens' confidence in the bodies ("deep structure"). In particular, a negative resolution should be justified persuasively and clearly when it comes to facts and the law so that there is no doubt that all circumstances of the case were deeply considered and evaluated and that the final resolution is their logical consequence.[192]

The judicial review also includes checking whether the application of the administrative discretion was admissible in a specific case. If the answer to this question is positive the court shall focus (considering matters discussed above) on checking whether the administrative body exceeded the limits of discretion. They are defined with laws in force, both in detailed provisions and in general rules already discussed. The court should examine whether the decision (or, specifically, its resolution) is within the limits specified in the law. If the legislature leaves freedom for the body issuing a decision to choose consequences only a particularly material (glaring) violation of the said framework of such discretion will constitute a violation of the law.[193]

Judicial review can also be expanded to include the verification of compliance with directives of the choice of consequences. The selection of a case resolution variant within the limits of discretion cannot be arbitrary. If a legal act defines the

---

191 Compare the ruling of the SAC in Warsaw of 26.05.1981, SA 810/81, LEX No. 11225; ruling of the SAC in Warsaw of 11.02.1981, SA 233/81, LEX No. 11205.

192 See the ruling of the VAC in Kielce of 19.03.2009, I SA/Ke 57/09, CBOSA.

193 See the SAC ruling of 7.11.2008, II GSK 455/08, CBOSA.

goal explicitly and the entity realizing that very act takes action not intended to achieve that goal one can assume that it acts in violation of the law and even with no legal basis. Therefore such actions are subject to judicial review. However, it is not (contrary to what one might expect) the review of purposefulness but rather the review of legality as the act is not verified from the perspective of off-legal goals but rather from the perspective of a goal clearly defined in the legal act being its basis. If such an act does not allow for the attainment of the goal defined in its legal basis it will be not only inexpedient but also contrary to the legal act.[194]

The multitude of rulings of Polish administrative courts referring to the method of making decisions as a part of the administrative discretion indicates that the issue is particularly important for the court from the perspective of the protection of individual rights from arbitrary actions of the administration. The influence of rulings of administrative courts on subsequent administrative decisions is mostly indirect and argumentative. The richness of judgments referring to the way of "using" the freedom of decision available to the body as a part of its administrative discretion offers important, unambiguous and categorical (supported by the constancy of the established ruling practice) indications in that area. Therefore, the ruling activity of administrative courts becomes a "signpost" (of a universal nature) for the reasoning of administering entities undertaking settlements as a part of the administrative discretion.

There is one more topic worth mentioning. The ruling practice of administrative courts reviewing decisions based on administrative discretion refers to fundamental operating conditions of the administration. By reaching for general rules and tasks of the administration, the court reviewing the compliance of administration's activities, in fact, determines boundaries between the purposefulness and legality by itself and the analysis of judicature's achievements shows that such a boundary is wide "for the benefit" of the legality and one can talk about constructing a legality of purpose here.[195] As the SC indicated in the ruling of 24.06.1993: "During the exercise of the judicial review of the legality of all discretional decisions of the administration (i.e. where the law offers a possibility for the administration body to valuate and select one out of varied resolutions permitted under the law), the role, tasks and scope of competencies of an independent court have to be understood more widely and more deeply than in other situations. To put it simply, discretionary decisions have to entail the intensified

194 See the ruling of the SAC in Kraków of 3.01.1995, SA/Kr 2937/94, CBOSA.

195 More: J. Zimmermann, *Polska jurysdykcja administracyjna*, op. cit., p. 122.

rather than a reduced judicial review conducted from the perspective of compliance with the law (law understood as the entirety of the system)".[196]

The control over the legality of a discretionary decision covers the review of its compliance with axiological values resulting from functional goals of an administration body.[197] According to W. Jakimowicz, the concept of the legality of the goal in the process of verification of decisions made as a part of the administrative discretion is supported, among other things, by the fact that "in its activities, the administration should not aim exclusively at the realization of individual legal standards with no consideration of goals assumed by the legislature in various of the expressed general directives or principles of the law".[198]

An interesting related thesis can be found in the SAC ruling of 9.03.2006[199] in which the court states that "when issuing a discretionary decision, a body is bound not only with the provision but also with the goal of the established provision and with ethical standards".

196 See the SC ruling of 24.06.1993, III ARN 33/93, LEX No. 10913.

197 More: K. Radzikowski, *Glosa do wyroku WSA z dnia 24 września 2004 r., III SA 1328/03*, „Przegląd Orzecznictwa Podatkowego" 2007, no. 5, p. 432. According to that author, such review will, in essence, refer only to the statement of reasons for a decision rather than its resolution (sentence).

198 See W. Jakimowicz, *Zewnętrzne granice uznania administracyjnego*, „Państwo i Prawo" 2010, book. 5, p. 52.

199 See the SAC ruling of 9.03.2006, I OSK 1267/05, LEX No. 198275.

Part IV. Macroscale of influence – administrative policies and governance processes vs. human rights

4.1 Judicial decisions and administrative policies

Policy, in the process of deciding within public administration, can be understood in various ways. One of them is the meaning of policy of administrative actions, deciding in the public sphere, which refers to adopted by the authority courses of action within their competence or referring to procedures in which things are decided in the sphere of their discretionary power.[200] It may, directly or indirectly, affect the choice of the type of action, its course, and the content of issued decision. It is stressed that the content of administrative policy is to identify – on the one hand – methods of legal regulation, and on the other hand, to determine the most effective ways (within legal limits) to achieve public goals. It relates both to the law-making, as well as the application of the law processes.

The policy of decision making can be understood as a certain way of performing tasks and, as a consequence, a way of acting in cases of a given type, or a way of managing resources that are available to the body. The policy of decision making can be shaped by different factors. One of them is previous decision of law application upcoming both from administration itself and judiciary. We are in fact talking about at least 3 different types of former decision *sensu largissimo*: previous decision of that single body, decisions issued by an appeal body (or generally speaking the body that is higher in the hierarchy and can somehow influence other bodies) and judgements of courts especially those which are responsible for verification of public administration actions.

Regarding the policy making, one may say that it can be created in a more or less intentional process of cooperation between public administration bodies especially in hierarchical subordination structures (which makes the influence of administrative precedents more noticeable) or independently, but still within the scope of the administration's organizational system. This means that

---

200 See more: M. Stefaniuk, *Działanie administracji publicznej w ujęciu nauk administracyjnych*, Lublin 2009, p. 113. This corresponds with the distinction made by J. Jeżewski (*Polityka administracyjna. Zagadnienia podstawowe*, [in:] *Administracja publiczna*, red. A. Błaś, J. Boć, J. Jeżewski, Wrocław 2004,p. 316) who distinguishes "policy towards administration" and "administration policy".

the administration sets detailed tasks for itself (which, in fact, complement the ones set by the lawmaker), as well as ways and methods of their performance. This, in turn, leads essentially to a more or less conscious activity. Consequently, decision-making borderlines are created, which are a result of certain internal guidelines or practices concerning the ways of dealing with similar cases. In the Polish legal system, public administration bodies do not have the competence to determine binding decision-making delineation for other bodies (to formulate specific "precedents"). Guidelines coming from the decision-making policy, regardless of the way it is shaped, the level of formalities and the motives that the body is guided by when referring to them, can influence the way in which the body uses the discretionary power it is entitled to, especially in relation to the decisions made within the scope of administrative approval.[201]

The influence of judicial decisions can be seen (as it was mentioned in part 2.3 of this book) as formal or informal. The first of them regards to situations in which, according to binding legal norms, administrative body is obliged to undertake a decision that was previously annulled by the court and, at the same time, it needs to take into account circumstances (factual and legal) pointed in the justification of such ruling[202] or even issue a decision of a specific content in accordance to court guidelines[203]. Informal influence applies to all cases in which the body is not legally bound by the indications made by the court. This influence can be noticed especially in relation to analogous (factual and legal similarity) administrative matters that belong to the competence of the authority whose previous decision was subjected to judicial-administrative review. In the Polish legal doctrine, it is indicated that public administration bodies, which decide in similar cases and who are afraid of repealing a decision, treat the content of previous decisions (administrative decisions or judgments) as "another part of the applicable law".[204]

---

201 A. Szot, *Stosowanie prawa przez administrację publiczną – między prawem a polityką*, [in:] *Zagadnienia stosowania prawa – perspektywa teoretyczna i dogmatyczna*, red. W. Dziedziak, B. Liżewski, Lublin 2015, pp. 205–217.

202 For example, according to article 153 p.p.s.a. "The legal assessment and indications as to the further proceedings expressed in the court's judgment are binding on the authorities whose actions, inactivity or lengthy proceedings were subject to appeal, as well as the courts, unless the legal regulations have changed".

203 For example, article 145a p.p.s.a – The law on proceedings before administrative courts, which gives the administrative court the right to issue a ruling instead of an administrative decision (after certain requirements have been met).

204 A. Błaś, J. Boć, J. Supernat, *Źródła prawa administracyjnego*, [in:] *Prawo administracyjne*, red. J. Boć, Wrocław 2010, p. 125. D. Dąbek, *Prawo sędziowskie w polskim prawie*

With respect to other decisions taken by public administrations, the greatest importance can be attributed to the decisions taken by bodies hierarchically higher than the decision maker. At the same time the analysis of the administrative decision-making practice within the Polish legal system shows the growing presence of judicial decisions in the justifications of administrative decisions, with almost no official reference to earlier administrative decisions. Judicial decisions influence public administration through their justifications by setting out some general "standards" on how to conduct the application of the law processes. This leads then to more general observation that stable case law (judicial decision lines) may influence the way public administration deals with cases of a given type. At the same time, the absence of a direct reference to them does not imply that the body did not take into account the "standard" indicated by the court. Due to the structural and political dependences of administration and the lack of its independence, we can observe the influence of this kind of precedent practice on the courses of action undertaken by public administration bodies within their competence or deciding in the scope of its discretionary power, i.e. shaping of administration policies for two kinds of motives:

1. pragmatic ones – positive assessment of undertaken actions and content of issued decisions by a court controlling administrative case and, in consequence, saving the time and (limited) resources necessary to re-address the decision in case of negative evaluation which may also affect the assessment of the body or its holder (chairman);
2. axiological ones – striving to ensure compliance of legal actions with legal norms and values of legal order and building citizens' confidence in the authorities.

The influence of judicial decisions can be seen in the strongest and most visible way in two phases of decisional process – the first one and the last one, namely during the pre-decisional phase, where the body will decide whether it is necessary (for the objective or subjective point of view) to begin the process and during the phase of formulation of final decision, especially in all situations in which the body will have at least minimum scope of discretion. Of course, this influence can be observed also at other stages but for shaping the administrative policies those two are the most important ones because those are the situations

administracyjnym, Warszawa 2010, *passim*; D. Dąbek, *Współczesne pojęcie źródeł prawa administracyjnego na tle konstytucyjnego pojęcia źródeł prawa*, [in:] *Koncepcja systemu prawa administracyjnego*, red. J. Zimmermann, Warszawa 2007, p. 91.

in which the body will decide what are the most optimal ways of acting in a specific type of situation.

Pre-decisional phase is the stage of the process of law application where the body decides whether to act – if there is a legal obligation to undertake certain actions or public administration body has a freedom in the scope of its discretionary power in this matter. In this phase, the body also chooses a proper form of action – law making, law application, other actions, e.g. information actions. Of course, this choice is often fully determined by the law-maker and the body will not have any freedom at this stage of the process because the occurrence of the fact which is relevant from the point of view of legal norm, will oblige the authority to take the actions indicated in that norm. However, in the legal system, there are situations in which the legislator makes the administration responsible for managing a particular sphere of social life without indicating specific obligations in this regard. Then, the body will be responsible for seeking the best way of doing so. Hence, it will first analyze the state of reality (factual situation) and determine the legal possibilities for different actions and then select the one that is the optimal, by the body's best judgment. Those situations can be very complex like, for example, the aforementioned expropriation process[205], which, according to Polish law, can be made if public goals cannot be implemented otherwise than by deprivation or restricting the rights to real estate. The pre-decisional phase will in this case cover a number of findings of the decision-making entity, including the existence of a public purpose and the search for the optimal way of its implementation. If, in the opinion of the administration, there is a need to make expropriation due to the impossibility of achieving the goal in another way, it will decide to initiate a process that is required. In this way, it will move to the decision-making phase of the law application process, in which it will indicate the property in relation to which it is to be expropriated, determine the right of ownership (or other relevant property rights) to these properties, etc.

In the future, in the situation in which this body will face the same problem in the similar state of affairs, those reasonings will be simplified and easier because the body will firstly verify whether the actions taken previously were effective and whether the current state of affairs can be re-activated. This argument will be stronger if an earlier decision had been approved or denied by a higher authority

205 Expropriation of immovable property consists in deprivation or limitation, by an administrative decision, of ownership rights, perpetual usufruct right or other right in rem. – See more Art. 112 of Polish Act from 21 August 1997 – on real estate management (*O gospodarce nieruchomościami*).

or court controlling the administration. So this is the way how administrative decisions lines are being created. The development of these administrative habits in the form of specific administration decision lines will influence the way the public administration body uses its discretionary powers and, in consequence, creation of administrative policies.

The final stage of the application of law process is the one where the final content of the action/decision is being formulated regardless of the type of the process. The influence of previous legal (judicial) decisions on the formulation of the final content of the decision will depend on the degree of discretion the legislature has left to the authorities and will vary. This influence is particularly noticeable in the cases of decisions based on administrative approval[206]. The construct of administrative approval is to give the administrative body the power to choose between two or more legally acceptable and equivalent legal solutions. This situation takes place when the legal norm does not explicitly define the legal effect of a factual situation but explicitly leaves the choice of such an effect to the administration. Of course, this choice is not arbitrary, in the sense that it must have a basis in the facts of the case, and take into account the directives of consequences selection. These directives can be divided into two basic groups, i.e. directives of the first order and second order (this will be discussed in more detail in the next part of this publication). The first of them are introduced by the legislator itself in the norm that gives rise to a decision based on administrative approval. The legislator may, however, give up giving the decision maker specific criteria that he or she should take into account when deciding. The impact of directives belonging to the second group is related to the influence on the decision maker and the content of the decision he makes, some extra-legal factors and values – structural and political ones, for example. And this is the place where previous decision (precedents) may influence the decision that is being issued. The decision maker is legally bound by the directives of the first group and, at the same time, it is directed in actual way by the second group of them.

Trying to answer the questions of influence of judiciary on shaping public administration policies at least few things are worth highlighting. Judicial decisions are mostly and directly present in actions of public administration as decision lines. On the one hand, it influences the later decisions of a single body

---

206 About administrative approval see more: M. Jaśkowska, *Discretionality, Margin of Decision and Administrative Discretionary Authority – an Attempt at Terminological Clarification*, [in:] *Discretionary Power of Public Administration. Its Scope and Control*, eds. L. Leszczyński, A. Szot, Frankfurt am Main 2017, pp. 15–36.

and on the other hand, those decisions create all together decisional lines that influence even stronger future decisions. In this sense, it influences the content of public administration policies. At the same time, this is only one of the factors that public administration has to take into consideration while deciding. As we consider decisional processes within public administration, one may say that most of them are being conducted in the situation of conflict (at least potential) of interests and arguments.

There are various reasons why public administration bodies follow or take into account previous judicial decisions but from the point of view of administration itself, the most important are the pragmatic ones. In most cases it is not about decision coherence as a value itself as it may occur in the judiciary, but rather as a decision coherence with certain extralegal arguments. This can lead to a situation that is referred to in the Polish doctrine as a reversed hierarchy of the sources of law.[207] The other thing which was not my field of interest is the question of whether administration should follow the decision lines from the point of view of an individual or the society as a whole. But one needs to remember that all public administration actions in the rule of law state must be undertaken on a basis of legal norms and in their framework which means that legal order (norm and values) sets the limit that may not be crossed ("holy borderline") of influence of precedential practice in public administration.

4.2 Governance processes vs. human rights – international courts influence (the ECHR example)[208]

As indicated in the previous parts of the work, public administration takes actions and undertake decisions in a complex legal, organizational, political and social reality, where a number of factors of a diverse nature affect the decision-maker and decision-making processes. All this leads to a situation of tension (aforementioned conflict of interests and values) in which public administration body undertake a decision of a specific content. In an extreme case, the impact of non-legal factors and impulses may be so strong that it will lead to an unlawful decision.

In order to counteract infringement of the law by the public administration, modern democratic states implement a number of solutions in their legal systems

---

207 See more: J. Zimmermann, *Prawo administracyjne*, Zakamycze 2005, p. 362.

208 See more: A. Szot, *The Influence of European Court of Human Rights' Jurisprudence on Public Administration Governance Processes*, [in:] *Global Governance and Its Effect on the State and Law*, ed. Martin Belov, Frankfurt am Main 2016, pp. 229–242.

that protect the individual from arbitrary, unwarranted or illegal decisions made by the administrative authority which can violate human rights. Some of those mechanisms were described in the second part of this book. Those national systems of control over public administration, especially decisions undertaken within the scope of discretion, should prevent aforementioned violations. However in reality many different situations appear in which such breaches happen anyway. As we consider the decisional processes at the national level and the relationship between public administrative bodies and the judiciary, at least three possible situations may occur.

In the first situation, the administrative authorities violate human rights and the court recognizes and prevents it. In this situation comes the elimination of the decision from the legal order or its correction (in terms of how competent the courts are in respect to such decisions), because of its incompatibility with human rights.

In the second situation, the administrative decision breaches the rights of its addressee and the court, for various reasons, does not prevent it. In this case, there is a breach of human rights and the national authorities responsible for the review of decisions didn`t oppose it and faulty (as not comply with law and human rights) legal decision or action remains in force and has certain legal effects.

In the third situation, the administrative body acts in respect to human rights but the court changes the content of the decision in a way that violates those rights. This is perhaps the worst possible situation, as it means the lack of proper preparation of the court (regardless of the reasons and motives for the court to change the decision) and probably in the most severe way infringes the principles of legal certainty and the confidence of citizens in the state.

The effect of the second and third situation is a legal decision that violates human rights that can be a subject of control of ECHR. For the state authorities and courts of the countries that have signed the European Convention of Human Rights (Convention for the Protection of Human Rights and Fundamental Freedoms and its additional protocols) the jurisdiction of ECHR is obligatory.

Therefore, the question arises whether the supranational system of human rights protection (namely Council of Europe system) can efficiently control decisions and actions of public administration bodies (even those connected with governance processes) and whether the system is sufficient to protect people from arbitrary decisions made by public administration. While trying to answer this question, it is necessary to look at the human rights protection system from two different perspectives: procedural and material.

The first perspective concentrates on the problem of whether the procedure before the ECHR makes it possible to verify decisions of state authorities, especially those undertaken in the scope of discretionary power. Often it can be difficult because the true motivations and reasoning of public administration bodies can by hidden under well prepared justification of a decision. However, the contradictory procedure before the ECHR allows each side to present its statement – first in the written version and then oral arguments. It allows individuals to point out to the Court issues that were, in their opinion, subject to violation. At the same time ECHR himself establishes the facts of the case and tries to answer the question whether human rights violation actually took place. The lack of procedural restrictions in this regard in conjunction with the contradictory process provides an opportunity to determine whether the decision of public authorities, even if taken within discretionary powers, have breached human rights.

The second perspective, the material one, is concentrated on the scope of the activity of the ECHR – the scope of its control. One needs to remember that the European Convention of Human Rights introduces general rules that are then developed into detail and specified by the judicial activity of the ECHR. The Court's jurisprudence permanently raises the standards of human rights' protection, which allows it to keep pace with the rapidly changing world and dynamics of social life. In this context, we can say that because of the judicial standards of the ECHR, the system is effective enough and can prevent further violations even in the situation of decisions made in the scope of discretion of public administration.

It should be pointed out that the subject of ECHR jurisdiction are cases where there already violation of human rights occurred and the judgement of the Court can only compensate the injured individual grievances or his or her losses. At the same time, however, the decisions of the ECHR have also to prevent human rights violations in the future, thereby enjoying a preventive function. The consequences of the judgments of the Court may be a change the legal provisions in state or changes in decision-making practice.[209] So as one might see the influence of jurisprudence of ECHR as an example of influence of international courts on public administration decision-making processes is both direct (decisional at the same time) and indirect (argumentative at the same time). The first one regards to a specific cases and decisions of an administrative body, which was the subject of ECHR control. The second one can be seen as more general one through aforementioned human rights protection standards. These standards

209 See judgment of the ECHR of 6.11.2007, Bugajny and others v. Poland 22531/05.

should be treated as interpretative guidelines by the public administration and thus (indirectly) affect the way of understanding and applying the administrative law.[210] ECHR jurisprudence acts as a catalyst for changes in national law and administrative practice, sometimes bringing about a strengthening of the scope of human rights protection.[211]

The case law of the ECHR influences the functioning of public administration and thus the governance processes, like national systems of court review of public administration, either directly or indirectly.[212] The direct impact is visible with regard to the specific case (decision passed by an administrative body) that have become the subject of the ECHR ruling. Indirect impact is associated with the formation of a specific line of decision-making and jurisprudence at the national level, based on the standards of the ECHR jurisprudence and mainstreaming judgments of the Court as an argument of interpretation or decision-making. The indirect impact through judgements of national courts that control actions of public administration body may concern the practices of the authorities of the state in which there was a violation of human rights but also other states whose case is not directly concerned.

The judicial decisions of the ECHR may affect the public administration and its activity at different levels.

The first of these, associated with direct ways of impact, is when the authority draws conclusions from its own case or cases carried out by other bodies in similar cases, and in which the ECHR passes judgement stating that a violation of human rights took place. This is a situation in which decision passed by specific administrative body was found to be violating those rights and was eliminated from the legal order. In this case administrative authorities should either act in order to undertake another decision in given state of affairs in accordance with human rights or take no activities at all because any action in this situation can be seen as a breach of those rights.

---

210 See M. Stahl, *Od obywatela do człowieka. Kilka refleksji w kwestii przemian w relacjach miedzy jednostką a władzą publiczną,* [in:] *Między tradycją a przyszłością w nauce prawa administracyjnego. Księga Jubileuszowa dedykowana Profesorowi Janowi Bociowi, red. J. Supernat, Wrocław 2009, s. 660 – 669.*

211 A. Redelbach, *Natura praw człowieka. Strasburskie standardy i ich ochrona,* Toruń 2001, s. 106–107.

212 M. Andenas, E. Bjorge, *National implementation of ECHR rights* [in:] *Constituting Europe - The European Court of Human Rights in a National, European and Global Context,* edt. Andreas Føllesdal, Birgit Peters and Geir Ulfstein, New York 2013, p. 225–234.

At the same time one need to remember that the content of a specific decision or the reasoning of decisional body can also be affected by jurisprudence of the ECHR in other cases similar to the one that are in the competence of administrative body. For example while recognizing a decision of an administrative authority acting in a specific area in the state the judgement of the ECHR can influence decision-making process of other administrative bodies acting in other areas of that state. In this sense one might say that administrative bodies follow the "precedent" (judgement) of the ECHR. What is more in some cases public administration authorities of one state follows the content of the Court judgement addressed to administrative authorities in other states. So some king of unification of decisional processes can be observed. What is more even if public administrative authorities from different states do not follow the case law of ECHR that is not addressed to them directly, certain level of unification can be seen because of introduction to the jurisprudence of the Court human rights protection standards that are identical for all states and their authorities.

On the second level, the influence of the ECHR jurisprudence on national governance processes involves taking into account by public administration (while undertaking specific actions) judicial decisions (line of jurisprudence) of national courts competent to review the decisions of the administration, the judgements of which are (to a lesser or greater extent) influenced by the judgments of the ECHR. On this level the impact of the Court jurisdiction is less noticeable which does not necessarily mean that it is less instanced.

The third level is the one in which the judicial decisions of a ECHR affects other supranational courts (for example Court of Justice of the European Union) or authorities, and those then become an argument in cases before national courts to verify the functioning of public administration. E. Benvenisti puts forward an interesting formula that the ECHR is a court that on an international level can be seen as an authoritative one and its judgments are a source of inspiration not only to national courts but also for judges and members of committees of other international bodies.[213]

The impact of the jurisdictions of the ECHR requires taking into meaning of the standards of human rights protection for decision-making processes undertaken by the state authorities. Those standards developed by the ECHR define the absolute limit for the activity of public authorities introducing a certain sphere of

213 See more: E. Benvenisti., *Margin of Appreciation, Consensus and Universal Standards*, "International Law and Politics" 1999, no 31, p. 843–854.

freedom of human, which (in principle) cannot be disturb by those authorities (at least without changing the national legislature first).

Thus, those standards can affect the reasoning of a public authority both in the decisions related to the exercise of unequivocal obligations as well as on management activities (connected with governance processes) of public administration. In this sense, it will affect the discretionary power authority on different stages of the decision-making process.

In the pre-decisional phase, it is linked to the question of whether or not the implementation of tasks set by public administration, in the context of human rights protection, requires any action. If the answer to that question should be "yes", it may influence the choice of one of the legally permissible methods to accomplish this task. In this context, for example, it is worth mentioning the proportionality principle which it is not stated at all in the text of the Convention, but only verbalized in the case-law of the ECHR.[214] The principle of proportionality requires that there be a reasonable relationship between a particular objective to be achieved and the means used to achieve that objective.[215] It is considered one of the most important legal principles under the Convention.[216] The proportionality principle, means "fair balance" between protection of individual freedoms and the interests of the general public.[217] The test of suitability and necessity (undertaken within aforementioned principle) can restrict the freedom of decisional body. Thus, the jurisprudence of the ECHR can be considered a kind of directive of choice of action.

The ECHR jurisprudence standards can also play an important role in the interpretation of law. As pointed out by B. Liżewski, interpretive arguments can help both in the interpretation of national legislation and in gaining a proper understanding of the provisions of the convention.[218] He points also to the

214 For example: ECHR judgment of 25.03.1992 Campbell v. The United Kingdom 13590/88; ECHR judgment of 13.06.1979 Marckx v. Belgium 6833/74; ECHR judgment of 26.04.1979 Sunday Times v. The United Kingdom 6538/74; ECHR judgment of 24.08.1998 Lambert v. France 23618/94; ECHR judgment of 07.12.1976, Handyside v. The United Kingdom 5493/72.

215 R. Clayton, H. Tomlinson, *The Law of Human Rights*, Oxford 2000, p. 278.

216 A. Kalisz, *Principle of proportionality as an element stabilizing the diversity of values in democratic societies (in the context of individual freedom)*, [in:] *Crisis and Quality of Democracy in Eastern Europe*, M. Jovanovic (ed.), The Hague 2012, p. 102–103.

217 A. Aleinkoff, *Constitutional Law in the Age of Balancing*, "The Yale Law Journal" 1986–87 96, p. 943–1005.

218 See more: B. Liżewski, *Operacjonalizacja ochrony praw człowieka w porządku Europejskiej Konwencji Praw Człowieka*, Lublin 2015, p. 403 and next.

legislative nature of the Court's standard, because it shapes the substantive understanding of individual human rights. In this sense, even in countries of civil law (continental) culture, adjudications become, along with legal provisions, a full-fledged source of law.

Finally, the judgments of the ECHR influence the final shape of decisions, particularly in cases where the authority is granted with the administrative approval construction. Then the ECHR standards can become one of the directives of choice of the consequences (directives that need or can be taken into account while passing the final decision) that the authority may (it is not legally binding so the body is not obligated to do it) take into account when making a decision. At the same time those standards determine the absolute limit for authority – for example, by eliminating one of the potential contents of the final decision, because it may infringe in some sense standards of protection of human rights. In this context one might say that those standards are limiting discretionary power of public administration even in the situation in which its actions are in accordance to the law.

In this regard, it is clear that the jurisprudence of the ECHR on the one hand limits the discretionary power of public administration in all decision-making processes and, on the other hand, directs the reasoning of a public authority.

One must remember that the introduction of the standard of protection of human rights does not presuppose its immutability, and most importantly does not prevent the autonomy of states that are high contracting parties to the European Convention of Human Rights. On the contrary, the Convention permits, with respect to certain rights, so-called limiting clauses (the concept of "margin of appreciation").[219] An example is the "freedom rights", which are characterized by being highly "axiological sensitive" and for which the ECHR cannot work out a uniform or acceptable standard with regard to their reference to morality or religion.[220]

---

219 See more: H. C. Yourow, *The Margin of Appreciation Doctrine in the Dynamics of European Human Rights Jurisprudence*, London, New York 1996; Y. Arai-Takahashi, *The Margin of Appreciation Doctrine and the Principle of Proportionality in the Jurisprudence of the ECHR*, Antwerpen-Oxford-New York 2001; the ECHR judgements: judgment of 20.09.1994 Otto Preminger Institute v. Austria 13470/87;. judgment of 22.10.1981, Dudgeon v. UK 7525/76; judgment of 21.02.2002, Ghidotti v. Italy 28272/95.

220 B. Liżewski, *Operacjonalizacja ochrony praw człowieka w porządku Europejskiej Konwencji Praw Człowieka*, Lublin 2015, p. 281.

The perception of the Convention as a living instrument for the protection of human rights, which should be interpreted in relation to the current needs and the specificities of the country allows for the flexible protection of human rights and relieves tension between national authorities and the ECHR.[221]

In this respect, it should be argued that the jurisdiction of the ECHR may significantly influence the decisions of public authorities, including those which are undertaken in the area of governance. In formulating standards of jurisprudence, the ECHR, at least to some extent, affects the development of uniformity in governance processes in the sphere of public decisions in states that have signed the European Convention on Human Rights. At the same time, it does not mean an absolute unification and is associated with certain minimum requirements in a democratic state while maintaining the autonomy and axiological individualism of specific countries and societies.[222] This happens regardless of how and on what level the decision of the ECHR affects public administration as well as the stage of the decision-making process in which this occurs.

221 E. Brems Eva, *The Margin of Appreciation Doctrine in the Case-Law of the European Court of Human Rights*, „Heidelberg Journal of International Law" 1996 no. 56, p. 312–313.

222 A. Kalisz Anna, A. Szot, *The General Clause: A Measure of Universalizing the Content of Law or An Expression of its Diversity? On 'Public Interest' and 'Public Moral' Clauses* [in:] *Legal and Political Theory in the Post-National Age* Frankfurt am Main 2011, p. 153–154.

Part V. Model approach

5.1 Rationalized administrative decision

Formulating conclusions and optimization postulates with regard to utilizing argumentation formulated in justifications of court rulings by administrative bodies on the one hand, and the method of communication of courts with public administration bodies on the other hand is possible when a reference point is defined, which will serve as a model to which the current practice in this respect is compared. In this publication, the model presented will be the concept of a rationalized administrative decision.[223]

A rationalized decision is a decision which is optimal in specific legal-economic-organizational-political and social conditions. In other words, this is the best decision possible in specific circumstances, not the best decision in general.

The concept of a rationalized decision assumes *a priori* its conformity to legal norms. A decision cannot be defined as rationalized if it is issued lacking the adequate power and in violation of a procedure, or if its content goes beyond the limits defined by the law. As already mentioned, discretionary powers mean such powers enjoyed within the law, and not outside the law. Similarly, a rationalized decision is a decision made in compliance with the law.

A rationalized decision is a decision which most closely fulfils the assumed purpose of a given action. It is not about complete fulfilment, as such may prove to be impossible to achieve due to various purposes of action which may be mutually exclusive, or due to the specificity of facts and the surrounding reality, or finally due to the fact that some purposes are defined in the form which requires permanent activity of the administration and will never be fully accomplished (e.g. ensuring public safety). At this point we need to remember that various factors may have impact on setting goals of administration activities. Such goals may be defined by the legislator as specific and explicit, which does not allow for any discretion to clarify the same, or may be defined with a certain degree of generality (required e.g. due to the dynamics of changes in a given

223 The concept of a rationalized administrative decision is described in greater detail in: A. Szot, *Swoboda decyzyjna w stosowaniu prawa przez administrację publiczną*, Lublin 2016, pp. 333–346.

social reality). As to the latter, clarifying goals of operation of an administrative body may be influenced by non-legal factors (such as political or organizational).

A rationalized decision is a decision which refers to all facts related to a case and which omits facts which are irrelevant in specific proceedings. It also implies the need of an in-depth analysis of each single case. Using paradigms in the decision-making process is aimed at speeding up the procedure, however it may not lead to issuing a non-rationalized decision as a consequence of mindless acceptance of such paradigms.

A rationalized decision is a decision which reconciles various (and frequently conflicting) interests revealed either before commencing the procedure or in the course of such a procedure. As indicated, administrative decisions are issued in a situation of a potential conflict of various interests. The role of the decision-maker is to identify such conflicts and define mutual relations, and finding collision in such relations, to resolve it for the sake of responding to one of these interests more fully.

Therefore, a rationalized decision constitutes a compromise, as far as it is achievable in specific factual circumstances. The need to take account of a party's interest, which is linked to the principles of an administrative procedure, and more broadly to the protection of human rights and freedoms, imposes a number of duties and restrictions on a body,[224] to which it has to adhere.

That being so, for a decision to be deemed rationalized, it needs to be issued following a discourse between participants of a decision-making process. At a minimum, such a discourse consists of an exchange of communications between two entities, i.e. the administrative body and a party to the proceedings. What is meant is a discourse *sensu largissimo* during the whole process of law enforcement and a discourse *sensu stricto* related to issuing and announcing a law enforcement decision.

Ensuring the right to comment on each piece of evidence to a party, possibility to put forward own evidence, possibility to get familiar with the evidential material collected for the case enables a party to express its views both in procedural and substantive matters in the process of enforcing law. A rationalized decision is a decision taken as a result of admitting free expression of views

---

224 Compare Z. Duniewska, *Geneza, charakterystyka i określenie prawa administracyjnego*, [in:] *Prawo administracyjne – pojęcia, instytucje, zasady w teorii i orzecznictwie*, Prawo administracyjne – pojęcia, instytucje, zasady w teorii i orzecznictwie, eds. Z. Duniewska, B. Jaworska-Dębska, R. Michalska-Badziak, E. Olejniczak-Szałowska, M. Stahl, Warszawa 2009, p. 58; ruling of the SAC in Warsaw of 26.11.1991, II SA 937/91, LEX No. 10323.

concerning the case by the party and the analysis of legitimacy of the accusations and statements formulated by the same. At the same time, it does not mean that a body needs to resolve the procedure to the satisfaction of a party or agree with each and every accusation or statement made by the same. However, it is necessary that it allows for a discourse, considers legitimacy of requests made by the party and addresses such requests.

Finally, a rationalized decision is a decision justified in the way which is effective in terms of communication. It means a decision which is an element of a discourse between a body and a party. Its contents should address the party's statements and the body's opinion in this respect, presenting arguments, especially if it disagrees with the arguments put forward by the party. A decision should be justified in such a way as to convince its recipient about its correctness. At the same time, it should be justified in a way which could open further areas of discourse, i.e. for example between the party, a body and a body of higher instance if an appeal is filed, or an administrative court or other potential discourse participants.

A rationalized decision is a decision taken and expressed in a way which enables verification of its correctness. Discretionary powers available to an administrative body (freedom to decide) are vested by the legislator. The impossibility to effectively verify the way of conducting the procedure and relevance of the final decision for their conformity to the above requirements would make the postulate to aim at issuing a rationalized decision illusory.

Finally, we should bear in mind that a law enforcement decision as an individual norm forms part of a legal system and as such cannot be in conflict with other "elements" of this system. In particular, it cannot be in conflict with legal norms and legal axiology expressed in legal principles. Such principles express values which a law enforcing entity should follow in its reasoning, including when choosing alternative ways of operation under discretionary powers. In addition, such a decision should not lead to conflict with other law enforcing decisions.

Understood thus, a rationalized decision needs to be deemed rational both internally (in the decision-maker's opinion) and externally (in the opinion of the party, a higher instance body, court or another observer). If a decision is not deemed rational in any of these areas it means that one of the prerequisites for a rationalized decision has not been met. What is also in favour of accepting this argument is the fact that the concept of a rationalized decision provides for its communicative effectiveness, i.e. it is deemed rational by discourse participants.

A rationalized decision means a decision which is most relevant, optimal, most completely fulfilling the assumed goal in specific conditions which take account of both legal framework of decision-making, legal, political and organizational conditions of operation of an administrative body, changing reality as well as features specific to a case. It is a relativized decision in terms of the system and the instrument at the same time.[225]

Such a decision is achievable by gradual reduction of discretionary powers at individual stages of the law enforcing process by eliminating alternative choices until the moment of making a specific decision. An administration body commences the process from the general definition of the operational goal and values to follow, then through limiting the alternatives to choices acceptable and relevant for a given case type (which entails rejecting other alternatives) moves on to taking action in a specific factual situation and choosing an alternative which is most appropriate according to specific criteria.

The set of alternative choices is limited by legal norms and principles, as well as facts of the case. The sources of choice alternatives may vary in nature and may be a consequence of the legislator's conscious activities, or may emerge in the way which is beyond the legislator's control. Elimination of alternatives within the discretionary powers attributable to a body takes place in stages. At the first stage, the range of possible choices is the widest. As the authority proceeds with subsequent reasonings in the decision-making process, it makes subsequent relativizations and gradually rejects the alternatives which meet the criteria preferred by the authority to a lesser extent. During the second stage, the discretionary power is relativized to the mid-range values or goals and the case type, and during the third stage relativization is strong in the context of a specific case within a given type of cases. The scheme of reaching the optimal decision in specific circumstances by gradual limiting of alternative choices within the discretionary power available is applicable both to the whole law enforcing process (broad sense) as well as decision-making during individual phases (narrow sense) which are connected with establishing the factual and legal status, classification reasoning and issuing a final decision and its justification, that is the discretionary power to make specific partial decisions.

The decision-making scheme within the discretionary powers available to an administrative entity proceeds towards gradual elimination of alternative choices, which automatically obliges such an entity to assume a reflective approach to its activities and decisions taken. As such, it excludes the possibility of fully automated procedure based on the conviction that if a given case belongs to a given

225 Compare M. Król, *Pojęcie luzu normatywnego stosowania prawa*, „Państwo i Prawo" 1979, no. 6, p. 71.

type of cases it needs to be handled in a specific manner. This type of intuition of an administrative body may prove useful during the first and second stage of eliminating alternative choices and in fact may substantially speed up the whole process. However, moving to the third stage, that is relativization with regard to the facts of the case, forces an administrative body to choose the decision from among the alternatives, which will be optimal in this particular case. This does not mean, however, that resorting to operational paradigms (customary activities) developed by a body so far is not possible. On frequent occasions, using such paradigms may simplify and speed up the whole decision-making process. The prerequisite for using such a paradigm should always be verification of its "validity" and "adequacy" with reference to a specific case. The specificity of facts in a given case constitutes an impassable limit of discretionary powers in law enforcement by administration bodies, and the basis for conducting any reasoning which leads to issuance of a law enforcing decision.

5.2 Court's influence on administrative decisions

Formulating conclusions as to developing a normative model of using the judgements of administrative courts should start from making a general statement that in the process of reaching a rationalized administrative decision the court may become a "guardian" and "navigator" at the same time. We need to keep in mind that a rationalized decision is a decision which most closely fulfils the assumed purpose of action, which complies with the values of the legal system (demonstrated in legal principles) and the binding legal rules, which reconciles various (frequently conflicting) interests, made as a result of a free discourse among participants of the decision-making process and justified in the way which is effective in terms of communication. Thus, the court will safeguard compliance of the whole process and its individual phases with the law. In principle, such supervision will be consequential, but at the same time preventive in nature (especially if a permanent ruling practice is developed). From the other perspective, going beyond the framework of a specific administrative matter allows for showing how the court should influence the discretionary powers of an authority, setting direction of reasoning in the process of eliminating alternative choices.

Through their judgements, administrative courts "hamper" the inclinations of public administration which, induced and targeted to action (on a micro and macro scale) by non-legal impulses, may intentionally issue a decision which is outside the legal system, and first of all in conflict with the binding legal norms and principles. Therefore, the court needs to be an impassable border for such type of activities by performing a thorough analysis. Supervising the administration within the limits established by the norms binding in a given legal system, the court constitutes an instrument for ensuring protection of human rights and freedoms against arbitrariness of the administration. By that, it becomes a crucial link of guarantee in a country governed by the rule of law. Administrative court proceedings in the course of which an independent court (non-subordinated and unrelated in organizational or political terms) verifies correctness of reasoning of an administrative body as to factual and legal findings, are the place where administration's activity violating the law has to be stopped. Here, the possibility to verify such activity also from the perspective of the criteria other than legality remains open. At the same time, the court has a greater role to play. It should not limit its function to correct fulfilment of its role as a guardian. It should assume greater responsibility, which is connected to showing administration bodies "the right path" to follow. We should bear in mind that, apart from the cases of intentional and conscious violation of legal norms by the administration, frequently administrative decisions may be issued against the law completely unknowingly and unintentionally.

The basis of each rationalized administrative decision is a sufficient level of knowledge of a law enforcing body, which comprises knowledge of the facts and the law. In fact, issuing a rationalized decision lacking knowledge of the facts connected with the case and the legal system (norms and principles) is impossible. Such knowledge is acquired through intentional education or more or less conscious process of informal learning. The element of this knowledge is to become familiar with and understand the environment in which the law (legal norms) and legal decisions issued based thereon (including law enforcement decisions) function. In the case of administrative bodies, this is the legal system *sensu largo*, which comprises i.a. the law enforcement practice – the jurisprudence.

Public administration and people who are a part of it are participants in a process of constant learning. This is a continuous and infinite process, which is a consequence of dynamic changes taking place both in the field of law but also in the surrounding social reality. This problem is highlighted in the studies on organizational aspects of public administration functioning, in particular related to creating organizational culture. One of such concepts refers to the notion of a "learning" or "intelligent" organization[226] as the one which is capable of searching for methods of adapting activities which are undertaken to the changing reality

226 More in: M. Stefaniuk, *Działanie administracji publicznej w ujęciu nauk administracyjnych*, op. cit., pp. 72–77 and references quoted therein.

based on the knowledge of new solutions and learning which expands creative potential.[227] In this sense, administration is capable of absorbing and using the absorbed and processed information to define its operational policy.[228]

The clash of the statics of legal regulations and dynamics of social life currently requires a new approach to administration processes in the state. In the opinion of representatives of the organization and management doctrine, operation of contemporary organizations (including public administration) is subject to two types of determination. On the one hand, solutions oriented to developing organizational learning skills are highly desirable, and on the other hand there exist values which reflect paradigms specific to a given organization.[229] These paradigms are defined as a "recognised and approved (generally implicitly) set of beliefs and assumptions within an organization with regard to the prerequisites for its effectiveness and viable operation".[230]

Judgements of administrative courts serve a dual role in developing administrative paradigms. First of all, they are the "source of knowledge" for administration bodies, in particular with reference to the proper way of understanding or the proper process of gaining understanding of the applicable legal norms. By means of justifications, administrative courts explain to participants to the procedure (administration body and the party/parties) provisions of the binding law or show how to conduct individual reasoning in the law enforcing process, in particular validation and derivation reasoning, in order to achieve an applicable norm which falls within the limits of such law, or more broadly the final decision falling within the limits of the legal system. Secondly, court verdicts themselves become the "source" of law in a broad sense (decision-related sense of sources of law), being a component of a broadly defined legal system. This means that a public administration body faces one more standard-setting fact which, even in the continental legal culture, will have impact on the content of the normative basis of a law enforcing decision in a specific case. In both senses, court rulings become an element creating the knowledge of the authority, which is necessary to issue a rationalized administrative decision. As the knowledge is expanded with additional information, which is not directly related to a specific

227 See: M. Stefaniuk, *Działanie administracji publicznej w ujęciu nauk administracyjnych*, op. cit., p. 75.

228 H. Izdebski, M. Kulesza, *Administracja publiczna – zagadnienia ogólne*, Warszawa 2004, p. 95.

229 M. Stefaniuk, *Działanie administracji publicznej w ujęciu nauk administracyjnych*, op. cit., p. 76.

230 J. Supernat, *Zarządzanie*, Wrocław 2005, p. 421.

decision-making process but may have impact on its reasoning (e.g. knowledge of the facts which are not connected with the case but may have impact on perceiving the reality by the decision-maker [broader context[231]], knowledge of previous law enforcing decisions [e.g. established ruling practice] or knowledge of the principles of a discourse), it is more likely to issue a rationalized decision.

At the same time, court verdicts will become one of the factors which have impact on the authority's reasoning related to elimination of alternative choices. The multitude of potential decisions, that is the number of alternative choices has its limits. If such limits are passed, it is not possible to deem a decision rationalized. The limits of possible choices determine the limits of discretionary powers, which on the one hand are guarded and on the other created by courts, because irrespective of the source of freedom, it is always limited by the facts of the case and the content of legal norms and principles. Within such limits, an authority should follow such preferences as to alternative choices which will lead to a rationalized decision, that is a decision which is optimal in specific circumstances. Various factors have impact on such preferences. Directing choices of the decision-maker, to a lesser or greater extent they influence his decisions. These are legal and non-legal factors.[232]

The first group can be defined as main factors. These are defined by the legislator in a more or less detailed manner in the binding legal norms. These are main factors in that a decision-maker is obliged to resort to them no matter what their form is. It is the duty of a decision-maker which results from the principle of the rule of law. These factors can be further divided into direct factors, which result from the norm creating discretionary powers and require consideration of specific criteria, and indirect factors resulting from other norms, which do it in an indirect way. Therefore, such a division is not based on the level of generality or detail of a criterion, but on the "closeness" of the norm creating discretionary powers. Indirect impact can be exerted by i.a. task-related norms or legal principles which do not define the criteria an authority should resort to but do it by referring to certain goals or values.

---

231 See the ruling of the VAC in Olsztyn of 15.01.2014, II SA/Ol 1166/13, CBOSA.

232 Such differentiation refers indirectly to the division proposed with regard to the directives of reasoning within administration's discretion by J. Wróblewski (*Sądowe stosowanie prawa*, op. cit., pp. 243–246) and M. Jaśkowska (*Uznanie administracyjne a inne formy władzy dyskrecjonalnej administracji publicznej*, [in:] *System prawa administracyjnego, vol. 1: Instytucje prawa administracyjnego*, eds. R. Hauser, Z. Niewiadomski, A. Wróbel, Warszawa 2010, pp. 263–264).

The other group comprises non-legal factors, which means that their sources are non-normative. We need to remember that "non-legal nature" may also be observed in main directives but with regard to references to non-legal values formulated in legal norms. At the same time, due to the localization of this reference in a legal provision, we need to recognize the authority's duty to resort to these values, which entails including them in the first group. Factors comprising the other group include the criteria the source of which should be looked for in non-legislative conditions of public administration functioning, such as organizational capacity of an authority or law enforcement policy.

Apart from different sources, the two groups differ in the authority's legal binding to apply such factors. The main factors bind a law enforcing entity by imposing an obligation thereon to consider specific criteria in the process of eliminating choice alternatives within its discretionary powers. The factors themselves may bind a decision-maker to a various extent; direct factors bind more than indirect ones. On the other hand, factors from the other group are legally unbinding and an authority is not legally obliged to resort to them. Legal binding needs to be differentiated from factual binding. With regard to the main factors, legal binding somehow "coincides" with factual binding, and an authority is legally obliged to consider specific criteria in the law enforcing process. The need to consider factors from the second group may be somehow consolidated with factual considerations, lacking legal binding of the decision-maker. It applies to the situations where the decision-maker's reasoning is influenced by non-legal factors to such a degree that an authority feels bound by the criteria resulting from such factors.

Court verdicts may be an element indirectly or directly shaping preferences of an administrative entity. The first situation relates to cases where an authority will consider court verdicts (apart from cases where it is legally obliged to do so) concerning (in terms of decision or arguments) the values of a legal system represented in legal principles. These principles, on the one hand, constitute an element of the decision-maker's basic knowledge, at the same time establishing limits of discretionary powers, and on the other hand a sort of "metarules" for choosing alternatives within the discretionary powers enjoyed by an authority. Legal principles serve as a "guardian" of rationality of the verdict. Representing values of a legal system, they limit the freedom of impact of non-legal factors on the preferences of a law enforcing body. By that they guarantee, as it were, that the decision will remain within the framework of systemic axiology. The other situation is related to cases where an authority will resort to previous verdicts due to the impact of non-legal factors. All pragmatic considerations related to the wish to avoid repealing the decision by way of court verification are exactly connected with the potential influence of political and organizational factors on the authority. Wishing to avoid a negative opinion about its operation, an authority will aim to minimise the situations where such operation (in particular its compliance with the law) could be questioned. In this way, rulings will have a direct impact on shaping the preferences for choosing alternatives.

As the Supreme Administrative Court (SAC) stated in one of its verdicts[233] "in executing its discretionary powers, if need arises, the administrative authority should spontaneously strive to learn all factors which should be considered in a specific matter, whereas it needs to act reasonably and justly, showing respect for the binding law".

5.3 Rationalization of an administrative decision by means of a discourse

As stated earlier, a rationalized administrative decision is a decision issued i.a. as a result of a free discourse among participants of the decision-making process and justified in the way which is effective in terms of communication.[234]

In the field of law, communication may be either one-sided or involve exchange of information. The first group comprises a monologue, that is a situation where a message is transmitted one-way, which is typical in particular of the law-making processes in the statute law culture. Here, communication is linear and asymmetric because the message is directed to an addressee whose position is significantly different compared to the sender (lower or inferior meaning subordinated), which in turn obliges the addressee to become familiar with the message and make an attempt to understand and conform to it. The communication where exchange of information takes place is represented by a dialogue and a discourse, which are examples of symmetric communication, that is a situation where the position of the sender and recipient is comparable and relatively equal and therefore they are co-authors of the message. That being so, a dialogue may be associated with such notions as a consensus, compromise, integration negotiations, mutual recognition or agreement, while a discourse is connected

---

233 See the ruling of the SAC in Warsaw of 30.05.2000, V SA 2568/99, LEX No. 48888. Compare the ruling of the SAC of 24.08.2010, II OSK 51/10, CBOSA.

234 This refers to the concept of R. Alexy (*Theorie der juristischen Argumentation. Die Theorie das rationalen Diskursesals Theorie der ristischen Begründung*, Frankfurt am Main 1978, *Communication and Evolution of Society*, Boston 1979) and J. Habermas (*Faktyczność i obowiązywanie. Teoria dyskursu wobec zagadnień prawa i demokratycznego państwa prawnego*, Warszawa 2005).

with convincing, proving, negotiating and rationality. On the other hand, a legal discourse is treated as a specific type of a practical discourse.[235] Thus, its rules are also specific, compared to general rules. First of all, which is highlighted especially by R. Alexy, such a discourse contains restrictions being in particular the result of the need to take account of the binding law. At the same time this allows for "limiting the number of possible rational solutions".[236]

Law enforcement processes in a discursive sense can be viewed upon from three perspectives – *sensu largissimo*, *sensu largo* and *sensu stricto*. From the perspective of the theory of communication, contemporary law enforcement processes *sensu largissimo* should be treated as complex communication processes where information concerning factual circumstances of handled matters or content of binding legal norms is transferred and processed in order to issue decisions which are later made available to the addressees and other recipients. *Sensu largo*, it is a set of communication activities of law enforcing bodies undertaken to steer the course of communication processes in a discourse *sensu largissimo* and aiming to control the activities of remaining participants during its course. In its strict sense, it is related to issuing and announcing a final decision which closes the procedure, and providing the statement of reasons therefore.[237]

The reasoning of a law enforcing entity is influenced by arguments formed by numerous participants of the discourse *sensu largissimo*, and depending on detailed legal solutions and actual conditions of the decision-maker's functioning some of them will be "stronger" than other. At the same time, the process of searching for an optimal solution forces considering each of such arguments.

The contents of individual partial decisions in a law enforcing process and its final result being the final decision should be the product of weighing the arguments formulated during the whole process by various discourse participants within the limits defined by the binding legal system. At the same time, decision-making in the situation of a potential conflict of interests requires adequate justification of the verdict which will be formulated in the way convincing to the recipients. The claim of justifiability should be referred both to the content of the final decision and a number of partial decisions taken during the whole process of law enforcement.

---

235 More in: R. Alexy, *Theorie der juristischen Argumentation. Die Theorie das rationalen Diskursesals Theorie der ristischen Begründung*, op. cit.

236 M. Zirk-Sadowski, *Wprowadzenie do filozofii prawa…*, op. cit., pp. 118–119.

237 More in: W. Cyrul, *Wpływ procesów komunikacyjnych na praktykę tworzenia i stosowania prawa*, Warszawa 2012, pp. 297–301.

A feature specific to law enforcement by public administration bodies is issuing an administrative decision within the administrative power of the decision-maker. This is reflected in the possibility to shape the addressee's legal status in an authoritative and unilateral manner. At a first glance, it may suggest lack of space for a discourse and marking this process of taking a legal decision with monologue features. However, such thinking is incorrect. While the final decision as such is a form of a one-sided statement of an authority (monologue), which is also characteristic of a court verdict, in the process of reaching its final shape the future addressee (party to the proceedings) has multiple possibilities (guaranteed by the law) to start a discourse with the decision-maker. Such a discourse is a natural consequence of values adopted in a democratic rule of law and detailed preferences (including axiological preferences) of the legislator.

Transposing these considerations to the Polish legal system, several issues need to be tackled if we wish to present the practical dimension of the analyzed phenomenon. First of all, the principle of active participation of the parties in the procedure[238] provides for the possibility of the party's participation in each stage of the procedure and addressing collected evidence and material as well as filed claims. Secondly, a number of detailed legal rules make the implementation of the aforementioned principle, and by that a discourse in the law enforcement process, real. To give an example, a party may demand the evidentiary process (art. 78 § 1 of the Code of Administrative Procedures), has the right to participate in the evidentiary process, has the right to ask questions of witnesses, experts and parties and to file explanations (art. 79 § 2 of the Code of Administrative Procedures), has the right to file explanations, documents and other evidence before the proceedings and the right to appear in person or via its representatives or attorneys (art. 80 § 2 of the Code of Administrative Procedures). In addition, in the light of art. 81 of the Code of Administrative Procedures, a factual circumstance shall be deemed to have been proven if a party has the opportunity to comment on the evidential process. A party also has the right to express an opinion on the entirety of the evidence and materials

238 More in i.a.: A. Matan, *Zasada czynnego udziału stron w postępowaniu administracyjnym w świetle orzecznictwa sądowego*, „*Roczniki Administracji* i *Prawa*: Teoria i Praktyka" 2005, pp. 103–120. See: ruling of the VAC in Warsaw of 15.04.2008, I SA/Wa 1812/07, CBOSA. The principle of legal certainty has also been referred to in the rulings of the Court of Justice of the European Union. Compare the ruling of 20.09.1990 in case C-5/89 *Commission of the European Communities v Federal Republic of Germany*, ECR 1990 p. 3437; the ruling of 20.03.1997 in case C-24/95 *Land Rheinland Pfalz v. Alcan Deutschland GmbH*, ECR 1997, p. 1591.

collected and to file claims before any decision is issued (art. 10 § 1 of the Code of Administrative Procedures).

Of course, an authority is not obliged to approve of each motion and request of a party, however it needs to become familiar with its arguments and then address them, and in case of disagreement, provide a thorough justification for its decision (in line with the principle of persuasion).[239] In this sense, an administration body becomes *de facto* the "host of the discourse" and is obliged to keep the party informed of the factual and legal circumstances which may have impact on establishing its rights and duties being subject to an administrative procedure. This is an attempt to overcome deficiencies related to the lack of adequate knowledge by a party to the procedure, which could affect discourse effectiveness.

The discourse between the body and the addressee of the decision does not need to end with issuing the law enforcement decision. Filing an appeal against first instance decision opens a new area for a discourse, and a party dissatisfied with the verdict may present its arguments in the appeal. In an administrative court procedure, this also entails the duty of the body to provide the court with the reply to the party's complaint together with complete documentation of the case (art. 54 § 2 of the Code of Administrative Courts Procedure). In this way the body is obliged to address (present its opinion) relevance of objections raised by the party.

The procedure before an administrative court is a model example of a legal discourse. Compared to other types of a practical discourse, it demonstrates a number of specific differences. In particular, the discourse has to end with an explicit decision made based on legal norms under the so-called procedural order to make the decision. Such a resolution is based on external rules and does not have to be accepted by all participants, although arguments of each of them are considered. The entity (audience) which evaluates effectiveness of arguments is the court. That being so, this type of a discourse is extremely limited by the provisions of the procedural and substantive law. Nevertheless, purely legal arguments based directly on the binding regulations constitute a sufficient basis for the decision only in relatively uncomplicated cases, that is such where

239 In the verdict of the SAC in Lublin of 20.11.2001 (II SA/Lu 629/00, CBOSA) the court stated that "[...] in order to implement the principle of persuasion, clear communication of the statement of reasons is required – diligence exercised in presenting to the addressee the justification of own arguments used in developing the decision content is an essential element of the persuasive function of the justification". See also: ruling of the SAC of 6.11.2007, II OSK 1393/07, CBOSA.

it is sufficient to read behavioural patterns from legal regulations and there is no need to choose between values. If we take a look at communication processes between the court and an administration body (let alone other "audience" and potential message recipients), several regularities should be mentioned.

The discourse between the court and public administration takes place mainly (or exclusively) by presenting a justification (both as an announcement made during the court hearing or in a written form developed following the verdict). On the other hand, communication between the body and the court takes place in several possible variants: (1) as a reply to the accusations of the party (addressee of administrative decision) raised in the complaint or an appeal against sentence (2) as arguments formulated in the appeal against sentence filed to SAC if a body fails to accept the resolution of VAC (the jurisprudence stresses that discursiveness is a prerequisite for an appeal against sentence[240]), (3) as a decision-making policy – the body executes the court verdict (VAC, SAC) in a given case and begins to do the same in other cases with similar factual circumstances. In the last case a situation is created where court arguments shape a decision-making practice in the administration.

The communication field (its scope and depth) in a discourse between the court and a public administration body depends to a large extent on the scope of discretionary powers which the latter enjoys in a specific law enforcement process. The greater the scope of discretionary powers, the greater the possibility to consider various arguments in the discourse, but at the same time also greater responsibility of an administration body which needs to evaluate and alternatively weigh such arguments, and provide a convincing justification for its decision. The discourse limits not so much the discretionary powers of a public administration body but arbitrariness of decisions taken, and forces the body to demonstrate the reasons which are in favour of adopting a particular decision. In this sense, communication forces rationalization of the reasoning of a law enforcing entity, and the arguments used rationalize the decision. At the same time, it needs to be noted that various factors of public administration functioning have impact on receiving and accepting court arguments by the body,[241] which include political, organizational, social and other factors. That being so,

---

240 See, among others.: the ruling of the SAC of 25.04.2008, II FSK 398/07, CBOSA; ruling of the SAC of 17.02.2010, II FSK 1525/08, CBOSA; ruling of the SAC of 5.11.2014, I FSK 571/13, CBOSA.

241 This refers to the convergent concept of communications – G. Gerbner, *Towards a General Model of Communication*, "AV Communication Review" 1956, no. 4, pp. 171–199.

the reasons for the potential approval or rejection of court arguments by the body are related not only to the correctness and relevance of the argumentation formulated in the justification, and the dialogue of the court with the administration may be disturbed by other external communications.

5.4 Impact of rulings on public administration – optimization postulates

The results of analyses of the law enforcement practice, both by the courts and the administration, which have been presented in previous chapters of this publication lead to the conclusion that formulating optimization postulates is reasonable. These will be conclusions presented in bullet points which, on the one hand, refer to the method of using court rulings by public administration, and on the other hand the way courts communicate with administrative entities.

In each case, public administration bodies should aim at issuing a rationalized decision, i.e. a decision which is optimal in specific circumstances. The rulings of courts verifying the activity of administrative entities constitute one of the conditions of rationalizing such a decision by, on the one hand, safeguarding the impassable limits of administration activities, and on the other hand contributing to knowing and understanding better the legal environment of making law enforcement decisions. Alluding to the previously mentioned concept of learning administration it should be noted that court rulings constitute an indispensable component of a decision-maker's knowledge which, in turn, is a prerequisite for issuing a rationalized law enforcing decision. At the same time, such a decision should stay within the limits of the legal system, emerge as a result of a discourse among various entities and be adequately justified in terms of communication. This leads to the need to formulate three optimization postulates concerning knowledge of, using and relying on court rulings by administrative entities.

The first (most general) postulate refers to continuous and thorough analysis of court rulings issued so far. This postulate is specifically valid for matters in the capacity of a given authority. Up-to-date knowledge of court verdicts and arguments presented in relevant justifications constitutes an indispensable element of knowledge of the decision-maker. At the same time, due to the number of potential rulings which administrative decision-makers would have to get familiar with in conjunction with the limited amount of time for fulfilling their duties related to managing a given sphere of reality, as well as frequent lack of legal education, this postulate will have to remain in the sphere of wishful thinking without realistic mechanisms for improving state of the art. In other words, it is not sufficient to make a general statement that each and every authority (and relevant officers) should become familiar with the current jurisprudence at least within the area of their capacity, even despite the fact that the vast majority of such rulings are available on-line (e.g. CBOSA [*Central Database of the Jurisprudence of Administrative Courts*] in Poland[242]). At the same time, in today's reality administrative decisions cannot function and be issued in isolation from the jurisprudence which (in the countries of the civil law culture) constitutes an element of the broadly defined legal system. That is why fulfilment of this postulate is possible by means of introducing appropriate mechanisms both, inside the authorities themselves and inside courts.

As to the authorities (the role of judicature in fulfilling this postulate will be discussed later on), this may happen by regular transfer of know-how to officers and sharing the knowledge of judgements in administrative cases conducted by various authorities, in particular within the same area and with regard to comparable facts. Fulfilment of this assumption may contribute to developing specific paradigms for procedures, and within a broader perspective to standardising the decision-making policy of public administration bodies, which in practice will translate into increased trust of citizens in the state and its authorities by fulfilling the postulate of certainty of and compliance with the law. The rulings of Polish administrative courts rightly point out, despite individual approach to each case, that delivering a different verdict with regard to entities demonstrating analogical factual and legal circumstances is incompatible with the constitutional principle of equality before the law and the principle of trust of the citizens in the state authorities.[243]

The above postulate is primal in relation to the remaining two in the sense that their full and adequate execution is not possible without executing the first one, i.e. providing the body (specifically persons in charge of preparing and issuing a decision) with adequate knowledge regarding opinions expressed in the rulings about each aspect (reasoning) of the law enforcement process, i.e. establishing facts of the case, validation and derivation reasoning, classification and issuance of a decision and its justification.

The other optimization postulate is connected with bolder and more frequent resorting to court rulings by public administration bodies. With the aim to ensure coherence of the legal system and issuing a decision which complies with the legal norms, it is necessary to treat court rulings as one of the normative

242 http://orzeczenia.nsa.gov.pl.

243 See ruling of the SAC of 20.10.2017, II OSK 1457/17, CBOSA; ruling of the VAC in Poznań of 15.07.2009, III SA/Po 60/09, CBOSA.

foundations of the decision or as one of the factors determining understanding of the norm to be used in a given matter. In practice it means taking into account court rulings in each case in the field of validation interests of the body. Obviously, their impact on determining norm contents will depend on detailed regulations applicable in a given legal system. In presenting the way of understanding a norm or determining its contents in their rulings, courts influence the way of reasoning of administrative entities not only with reference to a specific case which is subject to verification in court. Being legally or factually bound by the court judgement, a body will consider such findings in the law enforcement process conducted as a result of annulling earlier decision. At the same time, aiming to ensure consistency of its decisions and from the pragmatic point of view to keep in force subsequent decisions issued with reference to analogical facts, an administration body should resort to the arguments expressed in the statement of reasons of a verdict in other procedures. Consequently, it will lead to creation of specific decision-making practices and a broader administration policy. This, in turn, will positively contribute to the implementation of the legal system values mentioned earlier.

The third postulate refers to bolder and discursive, but at the same time real (factual) referring to court rulings in administrative decisions issued. In justifications of their decisions, administration bodies relatively rarely state whether and to what extent they have resorted to and used the arguments presented in earlier court verdicts. However, it is worth stressing that such a reference, providing of course that a body has actually resorted to the rulings issued so far, is reasonable and necessary both from the legal and pragmatic perspective. Justification of a decision should reflect the grounds used or considered by a body and make it possible to learn about the reasons for making a specific decision.[244] Grounds for a decision should reflect reasons and explain the course of reasoning leading to the application of a specific provision of the substantive law to the actual situation.[245]

244 See ruling of the VAC in Warsaw of 10.09.2008, VI SA/Wa 926/08, LEX No. 513863: "[...] justification the content of which does not allow for learning about the reasons behind the body's handling the case results in its being defective which justifies annulment of the decision since it cannot be controlled and it is not possible to assess its legality".

245 See ruling of the VAC in Szczecin of 8.12.2010, II SA/Sz 844/10, LEX No. 754972. See also ruling of the VAC in Warsaw of 3.03.2010, VIII SA/Wa 842/09, LEX No. 607086; ruling of the VAC in Warsaw of 19.03.2013, VII SA/Wa 2990/12, LEX No. 1321678.

At the same time, resorting to the jurisprudence is the use of an argument from authority, which strengthens the conviction that the decision is right. In addition, if it is later subject to instance or court verification, the chances for keeping it in force are greater.

However, we need to stress that this postulate is not about any, i.e. general and enigmatic relying on the jurisprudence or some unspecified ruling practice, but about referring to a specific ruling or a group of rulings together with recalling the arguments expressed therein which had impact on the process of issuing an administrative decision and the decision itself. It is not only about the "surface structure" of the justification, but about its "deep structure". The first one comprises a series of elements which are required in the justification by procedural rules, while the other one requires an analysis and specification of the assumptions and argumentation used in the decision and its justification.[246] When recalling the arguments from the jurisprudence, administration bodies have to show honesty, i.e. (1) demonstrate the justification to the addressees (the party, higher instance bodies, court, society) whether and to what extent they used court rulings and which rulings they used; (2) should not refer to the rulings which did not influence the decision.

Relying on the jurisprudence in the justification of an administrative decision should have the form of a discourse, if the body disagrees with the opinion expressed by the courts (this obviously does not apply to the situation of being legally bound by the court's judgement made in a specific case). A body should demonstrate why it disagrees with the arguments presented in the rulings or to what extent and why they cannot apply to a given case. Therefore, relying on court rulings in the justification of the decision should not be limited only to the situation of approving the same. This, however, requires greater courage of a body, supported with more in-depth knowledge (in this way alluding to the first postulate). In other words, the greater the knowledge of the arguments presented in the jurisprudence, the more possible it is to issue an optimal decision and provide a better and fuller justification thereof.

In addition, administrative courts themselves define in their rulings numerous "guidelines" regarding components of a justification in terms of its contents,[247]

246 More in: J. Wróblewski, *Decyzja sądowa a koncepcja systemu prawa*, „Acta Universitatis Lodziensis, Zeszyty Naukowe UŁ Nauki Humanistyczno-Społeczne" 1978, book 28, pp. 3–5.

247 E.g. ruling of the VAC in Kraków of 12.05.2009, II SA/Kr 340/09, CBOSA; ruling of the SAC in Lublin of 15.12.1995, SA/Lu 2479/94, LEX No. 27106; ruling of the VAC in Warsaw of 15.04.2008, I SA/Wa 1812/07, LEX No. 510335.

in particular with reference to decisions based on administration's discretion, which require the most thorough justification.[248] Within the limits defined by the legislator, the jurisprudence introduces standards which a justification of a decision under the rule of law has to meet.

Irrespective of the general guidelines above, it is justified in this respect for the administration bodies to develop internal rules (methodology) for using and recalling court rulings.

As to the second area, i.e. method of courts' communication with the public administration bodies, the postulates below should be formulated which on the one hand refer to the method of formulating arguments used in the statement of reasons, and on the other to the method of disseminating their content.

Firstly, it should be stated that courts should bear in mind that the direct addressees of justifications for issued rulings are both parties, i.e. the administration body and addressee of the administrative decision. The analysis of the history of rulings issued by Polish administrative courts shows the tendency to give stronger argumentation (which in certain aspects seems to be obvious) with regard to the party against which a ruling was issued. Regardless of the wish to convince this party of the "correctness" of the ruling, we need to remember that administration bodies "learn", i.a. by having their decisions assessed by external entities. Therefore, it is recommended that courts indicate not only mistakes made by an administrative body, but also reasoning and activities conducted properly. It is also justified that, especially in situations which are difficult and complicated in legal terms, more general arguments (apart from arguments related to specificity of a given case) are formulated which may constitute a guideline for subsequent cases handled by this or other bodies.

At this point, two postulates in particular should be formulated. First of all, in justifications of rulings courts should clearly indicate methods of conducting individual activities and reasoning by the authorities in the law enforcing process, and in particular with reference to legal grounds of a given decision. Secondly, which is a direct consequence thereof, courts should be bolder in attempting to indicate the values to which general referring clauses refer to. As indicated earlier in the publication, while administrative courts in Poland address the issue of

248 See ruling of the SAC in Warsaw of 19.07.1982, II SA 883/82, „CBOSA. See also ruling of the VAC in Warsaw of 26.07.2007, V SA/Wa 667/07, LEX No. 454405. Similarly ruling of the VAC in Warsaw of 25.05.2007, V SA/Wa 418/07, LEX No. 470110; ruling of the VAC in Warsaw of 22.03.2007, V SA/Wa 45/07, LEX No. 338239; ruling of the VAC in Warsaw of 7.11.2006, III SA/Wa 2015/06, LEX No. 328521.

decision-making within administration's discretion in a great detail, they hardly ever attempt to define the "content" of general clauses or at least indicate the way they do it or how administration bodies should do it. This is a visible deficit which may lead to the lack of coherence in the reasoning and argumentation provided by administrative entities.

Another issue is the need to make court rulings more discursive with regard to the arguments formulated by the parties to the procedure, as well as those articulated in court rulings. In this respect it is recommended, and even necessary, to show a bolder approach in resorting to the ruling practice and arguments articulated in other verdicts. This is aimed at showing whether and to what extent the judgements made by the court coincide with those already existing within the legal system, and to what extent they are different. At the same time, similarly to the need to make justifications of administrative decisions more discursive, substantiating the legal grounds for a ruling cannot consist of presenting a lengthy list of examples of reasoning adopted in rulings without the court's expressing its opinion thereon. The court needs to refer such judgements to a specific case which is being analyzed.[249] Departing from the existing or prevailing argumentation practice requires a particularly detailed justification, because a court verdict which is outside this scope is likely to become a precedent which will be a starting point for a new practice both for court rulings and decisions of administration bodies.

However, if this is to happen, contents of a ruling need to reach a broader group of addressees of the justification of such a court verdict. In particular, we have in mind administration bodies other than the one whose decision was appealed against. Thus, moving to postulates regarding disseminating information about arguments expressed in the jurisprudence, it is worth recalling a postulate formulated with regard to utilizing court rulings by the public administration, which is related to the constant and detailed analysis of the history of court rulings, and it should be stated that not only administrative entities but also courts should be involved in its implementation to the fullest extent possible. It is justified to develop effective mechanisms, irrespective of making full content of all issued rulings publicly available, which make it possible to gather and share knowledge of the rulings or judgements and arguments expressed therein, which are of key importance from the point of view of functioning of administrative bodies. An undeniable fact is that court rulings have a direct and indirect

249 More in: B. Dauter, *Metodyka pracy sędziego sądu administracyjnego*, Warszawa 2011, p. 461.

impact on the reasoning of administrative entities and decisions they issue, and therefore it is even more justified for the courts to assume greater responsibility in this respect, which at the same time makes the decision-making activity of administration bodies easier and contributes to maintaining greater coherence within the legal system and to better protection of rights of individuals against any possible violation of the law by administration. Court rulings should thus serve as a "motivator" and a "signpost" steering the reasoning of public administration bodies, and at the same time as a "brake" suppressing the temptation to issue a decision against the law, or minimising the risk of issuing such a decision by mistake, while the court should be a "guardian" and "navigator".

Conclusion

Deliberations in this publication confirmed preliminary research hypotheses regarding the existence of feedback between administrative courts and bodies of public administration controlled by them. Legality verification of activities by the latter is not, however, limited to "simply" stating that this requirement, fundamental in the country governed by laws, is met or not. This is connected, in each case, with their confrontation with legal and other axiology. Court rulings may have various effects, i.e. "depth", "width" and "intensity" of impact, both on individual decision-making processes in public administration and in formulation of decision-making approach (administration policies) understood as behavioural routines (habits) for acting in certain cases. The force of court impact on administrative decision depends most of all on how much the body of administration is bound with court ruling, either direction of resolution or arguments expressed in the substantiation.

The analysis of Polish legacy judicature and legal doctrine enabled establishing the descriptive model of court ruling impact on reasoning of public administration bodies in law application processes and the shape of final decision. This model demonstrates such phenomena in micro scale, i.e. referred to individual decision-making process, and in macro-scale, i.e. referring to administrative decision-making policies and protection of human rights. The research demonstrated that system of court control of decision-making process under the freedom of decision granted to bodies of public administration is on the one hand the intransgressible borderline of public administration activities, and on the other hand one of the factors determining decision-making process, and that if affects both the extent of such decision-making process, be reducing the area of freedom and focusing the reasoning of decision-makers.

Descriptive model of manner and extent of administrative courts' ruling impact on law application decisions issued by bodies of public administration was used, in comparison with models of court control over public administration functioning in sleeted European countries, as the base for formulation of optimization postulates (normative model). The concept of "rationalized law application decision", which assumes that bodies of public administration shall pursue in their actions the issuance of rational decision, understood as not the best possible decision, but the best possible decision under circumstances, was used as the starting point. Such circumstances refer to features of the specific actual conditions of the case, legal system form at the moment of decision-making, and values giving the base for such system, efficiency considerations of administration functioning, and social and political values preferred at that time. When the decision accounts for such circumstances and was worked in the discourse between various stakeholders of the broadly understood law application debate, it should meet the optimality requirement.

In this concept administrative judicature plays a double role. On the one hand it becomes a "guardian", whose vigilance shall prevent possible infringement (whether intentional or not) of legal standards, in and by activities of public administration. Court is a *de facto* protector of lawfulness and legal security. It shall perform this function both vis-a-vis individual decisions (follow-up nature of sentences), as well as the series of other decisions made under similar (but not necessarily) actual conditions by this and other bodies (preventive nature of sentences). On the other hand, court becomes a "navigator" for "learning" public administration. Pointing in the content of their rulings to specific directions of action and reasoning referring either to the essence of (legal and substantial) phenomena learned, or to manners in which pubic administration should learn such phenomena, it affects the reasoning of law applying entity. Court sentences comprise the fundamental knowledge of decision-maker and as such they become one of arguments for selection from various alternatives, under the freedom of decision.

In this context, communication between the body of administration and procedure stakeholders as well as other recipients of the substantiation content, including courts controlling their activity, as well as feedback from court, becomes of critical significance. Communication and discourse are among fundamental considerations in the issuance of rationalized administrative decision. This in turn was the starting point for formulation of optimization postulates as regards on the hand using by public administration legacy court rulings, and on the other hand communication between courts and administration. In addition to comments in section 5.4 referring to this area, it is also worth pointing out that methodology in this area needs to be developed, both by administration and by courts. Thus, meta-level communication and discourse are required, to enable working out (even non-formalized and postulative) guidelines in this important area.

To be honest to the reader, it is worth to mention that the model presented was built on the foundation of analyses of administrative decision-making process under the democratic legal order of the country governed by laws. It is, however, universal and may be applied in each political system, including during system transformation phase caused by deep social change. Critical condition precedent is, however, the existence of independent courts.

Finally, the author wants to express hope that deliberations in this study shall be the base for further research in the subject area, including inquiries undertaken by other researchers, and that their critical assessments shall increase the awareness of complexity of processes of law application by bodies of public administration, which shall translate into better quality of activities taken by such entities.

Lex et Res Publica
Polish Legal and Political Studies

Edited by
Anna Jarón

Vol. 1 Anna Jarón: Socio-Economic Constitutional Rights in Democratisation Processes. An Account of the Constitutional Dialogue Theory. 2012.

Vol. 2 Stanisław Filipowicz: Democracy – The Power of Illusion. 2013.

Vol. 3 Teresa Dukiet-Nagórska (ed.): The Postulates of Restorative Justice and the Continental Model of Criminal Law. As Illustrated by Polish Criminal Law 2014.

Vol. 4 Agnieszka Kupzok: Enforcement of Patents on Geographically Divisible Inventions. An Inquiry into the Standard of Substantive Patent Law Infringement in Cross-Border Constellations. 2015.

Vol. 5 Alicja Jagielska-Burduk / Wojciech Szafrański: Legal Issues in Cultural Heritage Management. A Polish Perspective. 2016.

Vol. 6 Maciej Mataczyński (ed.): The Takeover of Public Companies as a Mode of Exercising EU Treaty Freedoms. 2017.

Vol. 7 Maciej Barczewski (ed.): Value of Information. Intellectual Property, Privacy and Big Data. 2018.

Vol. 8 Pawel Smoleń, Marcin Burzec: Introduction to Polish Tax Law. 2018.

Vol. 9 Łukasz Pohl, Konrad Burdziak: Judicial Interpretation of the 1997 Criminal Code Provisions on Self-Defence. 2019.

Vol. 10 Adam Szot: Judicial Review of Administrative Discretion. The Influence of Court Decisions on Administrative Actions. 2019.

www.peterlang.com